𝔗𝔥𝔢 𝔒𝔵𝔣𝔬𝔯𝔡 𝔐𝔞𝔫𝔲𝔞𝔩𝔰 𝔬𝔣 𝔈𝔫𝔤𝔩𝔦𝔰𝔥 𝔥𝔦𝔰𝔱𝔬𝔯𝔶
Edited by C. W. C. OMAN, M.A., F.S.A.

No. III

ENGLAND
AND THE
HUNDRED YEARS' WAR
(1327—1485 A.D.)

BY

C. W. C. OMAN, M.A., F.S.A.
FELLOW OF ALL SOULS COLLEGE
AUTHOR OF "THE ART OF WAR IN THE MIDDLE AGES"
"WARWICK THE KING-MAKER", ETC.

The Naval & Military Press Ltd

Published by

The Naval & Military Press Ltd
Unit 5 Riverside, Brambleside
Bellbrook Industrial Estate
Uckfield, East Sussex
TN22 1QQ England

Tel: +44 (0)1825 749494

www.naval-military-press.com
www.nmarchive.com

In reprinting in facsimile from the original, any imperfections are inevitably reproduced and the quality may fall short of modern type and cartographic standards.

GENERAL PREFACE.

There are so many School Histories of England already in existence, that it may perhaps seem presumptuous on the part of the authors of this series to add six volumes more to the number. But they have their defence: the "Oxford Manuals of English History" are intended to serve a particular purpose. There are several good general histories already in use, and there are a considerable number of scattered 'epochs' or 'periods'. But there seems still to be room for a set of books which shall combine the virtues of both these classes. Schools often wish to take up only a certain portion of the history of England, and find one of the large general histories too bulky for their use. On the other hand, if they employ one of the isolated 'epochs' to which allusion has been made, they find in most cases that there is no succeeding work on the same scale and lines from which the scholar can continue his study and pass on to the next period, without a break in the continuity of his knowledge.

The object of the present series is to provide a set of historical manuals of a convenient size, and at a very moderate price. Each part is complete in itself, but as the volumes will be carefully fitted on to each other, so that the whole form together a single continuous history of England, it will be possible to use any two or more of them in successive terms or years at the option of the instructor. They are kept carefully to the same scale, and the editor has done his best to put before the various authors the necessity of a uniform method of treatment.

The volumes are intended for the use of the middle and upper forms of schools, and presuppose a desire in the scholar to know something of the social and constitutional history of England, as well as of those purely political events which were of old the sole staple of the average school history. The scale of the series does not permit the authors to enter into minute points of detail. There is no space in a volume of 130 pages for a discussion of the locality of Brunanburgh or of the authorship of *Junius*. But due allowance being made for historical perspective, it is hoped that every event or movement of real importance will meet the reader's eye.

All the volumes are written by resident members of the University of Oxford, actively engaged in teaching in the Final School of Modern History, and the authors trust that their experience in working together, and their knowledge of the methods of instruction in it, may be made useful to a larger public by means of this series of manuals.

CONTENTS

Chap.		Page
I.	From the Accession of Edward III. to the Fall of Mortimer, 1327-1331,	7
II.	From the Fall of Mortimer to the Outbreak of the Struggle with France. The Scottish War. 1330-1337,	15
III.	The First Stage of the Hundred Years' War, 1337-1349. From the Outbreak of War to the Black Death,	25
IV.	From the Black Death to the Peace of Bretigny, 1349-1360,	43
V.	From the Peace of Bretigny to the Renewal of the French War.—England under Edward III.—The Spanish War. 1360-1369,	54
VI.	The Last Years of Edward III., 1369-1377—The Loss of Aquitaine—Domestic Troubles—Rise of the Wycliffites,	65
VII.	Richard II. The Years of the Minority, 1377-1388,	77
VIII.	Richard II., 1388-1399,	88
IX.	Henry IV., 1399-1413,	96
X.	Henry V., 1413-1422,	105
XI.	Henry VI. The Minority and the French War, 1422-1450,	116
XII.	The Wars of the Roses, 1450-1464,	126
XIII.	Richard the King-maker and Edward the King, 1464-1483,	140
XIV.	Richard III., 1483-1485,	150
	Index,	163

Map of England,	6
Plan of Crécy,	37
Plan of Poictiers,	48
Map of France in 1360,	52
Plan of Agincourt,	110
The French Succession,	24
The Breton Succession,	32
The White Rose and the Nevilles,	160
The Red Rose,	161

ENGLAND AND THE HUNDRED YEARS' WAR

(1327—1485 A.D.)

CHAPTER I.

FROM THE ACCESSION OF EDWARD III. TO THE FALL OF MORTIMER, 1327–1331.

On the seventh of January, 1327, the Parliament of England, duly assembled at Westminster, declared that their king, Edward of Carnarvon, was deposed, and that they had chosen in his stead his eldest son, Edward Prince of Wales, to fill the vacant throne. In all the long annals of the nation no reign has ever commenced under such shameful auspices as the fifty years' rule of King Edward III. His miserable shiftless father had been deposed not so much by the will of the nation as by the private enmity of an unfaithful wife and a faction of disloyal barons. He had perhaps deserved to lose his crown, but not by such means, nor at the hands of such enemies. Moreover, heavy as is the guilt which rests on the conspirators who dethroned him, the nation must take its share in the blame. The mass of the baronage and the people stood aside while Queen Isabella and her adherents worked their wicked will on the king and his friends, and hardly a voice was raised to protest against the violence and cruelty which accompanied the revolution. The mob of London made itself the accomplice of the traitors by tearing to pieces Bishop Stapleton of Exeter, one of the late monarch's few faithful followers.

Deposition of Edward II.

No complaint was made in Parliament concerning his murder, nor concerning the equally illegal execution of the Earl of Arundel and the two Despencers, whom the queen had slain without due process of law. No one protested, save four courageous prelates, when the wretched time-serving Archbishop Reynolds cried aloud that "the voice of the people was the voice of God", and pretending to take the cries of a noisy faction for the fiat of heaven, saluted the young Edward of Windsor as his king. So with surroundings of the basest cruelty, hypocrisy, and cowardice, the new reign began.

Of those whose names appear in the shameful business of the fall of Edward II., the young boy in whose behalf the transaction was nominally carried out must bear the least blame. The new king was only fourteen years and two months old at his accession, having been born on November 13th, 1312. He had been neglected by his father, and had been of late in his mother's hands. There is no reason to believe that he suspected the cause which lay at the bottom of her actions, the hatred which she felt for her husband since she had become infatuated with the handsome, unscrupulous exile, Roger of Mortimer. In after years we know that he felt bitter shame for the way in which he had been made the tool of his mother and her paramour. Meanwhile he accepted the situation, and freely set his hand to all the documents and deeds which they laid before him. He seems to have shown no anxiety about the fate of his father, when the dethroned king was removed from Kenilworth to Berkeley Castle, and put under gaolers who were bent on compassing his death. Of the sinister purpose of the transference he had no suspicion.

To guide the steps of the young king the Parliament, in January, 1327, appointed a Council of Regency of four earls, four bishops, and six barons. But from the first the real power lay in the hands of Queen Isabella, whose word was all-powerful with her son. Behind Isabella, unseen at first, but growing more and more evident as the months rolled

Mortimer's predominance.

on, was the will and influence of her favourite Mortimer. They kept the young Edward in their hands, secluded him as much as possible from intercourse with those who were not of their own faction, and endeavoured to the best of their ability to distract him from affairs of state. It was long before the baronage and the nation realized the true condition of affairs, and longer still before the king awoke to a consciousness of the shameful tutelage in which he was living.

At first public affairs were conducted with some decent semblance of constitutional government. The old charters of the realm were confirmed, lavish promises of good government were made to Parliament, and the persons who had been attainted in the reign of Edward II. were restored to their honours and estates. Mortimer's power was not yet openly shown, and moreover a new danger soon arose to distract the nation's attention. Less than three months after the young king's accession the Scots broke the truce which had been concluded with them in the year 1323, and came flooding over the border into Northumberland and Durham, savagely wasting the whole countryside as far as the Wear and the Tees. King Robert Bruce was no longer at their head— he was already stricken down by the leprosy of which he afterwards died; but two of his old companions in arms, Sir James Douglas and Randolf Earl of Murray, were leading the raiders—twenty thousand moss-troopers mounted on light Galloway nags—and showed themselves quite capable of carrying out their master's usual tactics.

To repel this invasion the young king himself took the field; Mortimer accompanied him, for he never let Edward stir far from his side. The whole feudal host and shire-levies of England followed them, but no good fortune attended their march. The Scots were found waiting behind the Tyne in a post too strong to be attacked in front; when the English by a toilsome march turned their flank, the agile enemy was found to have already decamped, and to have fallen back on a second position as strong as the first. Mortimer would not risk an attempt to storm it—the memory of Bannockburn was still fresh in English memories—and again when he proceeded to move round to cut off the invaders from their retreat, Douglas avoided him by a night march and was in safety long ere his slowly-moving enemy had reached the point of vantage. So Edward's army followed the Scots for a time, always arriving too late, and always finding nothing but blazing villages and slaughtered cattle to show where the foe had been. The only striking incident in the campaign was a night attack which Douglas made with a small party on the royal camp. He cut his way far among the tents, and almost captured the young king, whose chaplain was slain in the scuffle; then he turned back and escaped unharmed. When the Scots were far on their way towards the Tweed, the English gave up the pursuit, and returned to Newcastle, utterly foiled and nearly starved by their long wanderings on the Northumbrian moors. Such was the inglorious introduction to war of the future victor of Sluys and Crecy. [Aug.–Sep., 1327.]

Renewed war with Scotland.

It was perhaps in consequence of this shameful failure to cope with the Scots, and in fear of the discontent that it might breed against the new government, that the queen and Mortimer resolved to murder the dethroned king. The strong constitution of Edward II. had resisted the harsh treatment and cruel privations to which he had been exposed in his prison at Berkeley. Finding that he did not show any signs of dying, they resolved to put an end to him. Their creatures were introduced into the castle at night, and secretly slew him [Sep. 21, 1327]. His death was long concealed, and when it was divulged was attributed to natural causes, or a broken heart.

Murder of Edward.

Another such campaign as the last, which recalled the worst misadventures of the reign of the late king, would have ruined the credit of the new government. Accordingly the queen and Mortimer resolved to make peace at any price with the Scots. Negotiations with the Bruce were carried on all through the winter of 1327–8, and, since the English were resolved on coming to terms, reached a successful issue. By the Treaty of Northampton, which men called "The Shameful Peace", the independence of the northern realm was fully conceded (May 4, 1328). Edward was made to sign away all claims of feudal superiority of any kind over Scotland, so that for the first time since Anglo-Saxon days the King of Scots could call himself without dispute a wholly independent sovereign. The Scottish regalia and royal treasures, together with the records of the realm, which Edward I. had brought to London, were restored: with them would have gone the famous "Stone of Scone", which still lies under the throne in Westminster Abbey, if a mob of Londoners had not fallen upon the workmen who were removing it. The King of England also promised to give his sister Joan, a little girl of seven, in marriage to Bruce's young son David. The Scots, on the other hand, promised to restore to their estates the barons of their realm who had been exiled for adhering to the English party, and to pay £20,000 in three instalments in satisfaction for all claims for damage and compensation for the harm which they had done in their many raids into England.

The Peace of Northampton.

It was only when the danger from the Scottish war had been thus staved off that Mortimer began to show openly his haughty temper and his disregard of the laws. He got himself created Earl of March, and took upon him such state as no subject of the realm had ever before dared to display. A hundred and eighty men-at-arms followed him wherever he went, and were used to overawe any of the barons who showed a wish to oppose him. At the Parliament of Salisbury, in the autumn of 1328, he came with so many armed followers at his back that most of the other peers, who had been bidden to attend without large retinues, fled away to Winchester, fearing that they were about to be seized and imprisoned. Moreover, men began to take note of his relations with the queen; they were so much together and so familiar in their intercourse that the truth began to be suspected.

Nevertheless it was to be three years before the favourite was overthrown, and ere his fall he was to do much more evil. Among the young king's nearest relatives were his two half-uncles Edmund Earl of Kent, and Thomas Earl of Norfolk, the sons of the second marriage of Edward I. These two princes joined with Henry Earl of Lancaster, who had done so much to overthrow the late king, in resenting Mortimer's influence. They felt that they, and not this upstart who ruled by the queen's favour, ought to have the final word in the governance of the realm. Kent took the lead, and drew upon himself the main brunt of Mortimer's anger. A disgraceful plot was laid to compass his destruction: he was secretly informed that his brother Edward II. was still alive, kept in strict confinement in Corfe Castle. Such corroboration to the story was furnished by the governor of the place, that Kent was fully persuaded of its truth, and wrote letters to his supposed brother, in which he proposed to free him and replace him on the throne. The documents were promptly passed on to Mortimer, who, when they were once in his hands, seized Kent's person, tried him for high treason, and had him beheaded the moment that he was condemned. The young king was induced to set his hand to the death-warrant by being told that his uncle's plan included his own murder by poison. Only eight days elapsed between the arrest and the execution, so that Kent's friends had no time to attempt anything in his behalf. [March, 1330.] Mortimer seized upon his victim's lands, which, added to the plunder of the Despencers, which was already in his hands, made him almost the wealthiest personage in the realm.

Execution of the Earl of Kent.

Kent had been well liked by the baronage and people; he was a courteous, kindly, and liberal prince, against whom no one bore any grudge. Hence his fate provoked bitter murmurings, and awoke the nation to a sense of its disgraceful plight. The guilty relations of the queen and Mortimer were growing daily more evident as long impunity made them less cautious. The true story of the

THE KING OVERTHROWS MORTIMER. 13

death of Edward II. was also beginning to be bruited about. Hence discontent grew every day more marked, and Mortimer's cruel plot against Kent may be said to have brought about his own ruin. When men began to ask each other whether the late king had been dethroned merely in order that a vicious Frenchwoman and a bloodthirsty upstart might rule England at their will, it was evident that the end was drawing near.

The blow, however, was not to be dealt by any popular rising, but by an unexpected hand. The young king himself was at last moved to action. For more than three years he had let himself be led by his mother and Mortimer, but at last he was developing a will of his own. He was now eighteen, had married a wife, the fair and virtuous Philippa of Hainault, and had just become the father of a son—Edward, so well known afterwards as the "Black Prince". He at last began to use his own eyes, and to take counsel of others than his mother's partisans. Gradually he began to realize that he was but the tool of Mortimer. Accordingly he prepared to make an end of this state of things.

In October, 1330, the Court was staying at Nottingham, and the queen and Mortimer lay in the castle, whose gates were well guarded by their retinue. But the king opened his purpose to the governor, Sir William Eland, who feared to disobey him, and consented to show him a secret passage by which he could enter without rousing Mortimer's followers. At midnight Edward, accompanied by his friend William, Lord Montacute,[1] and a few more armed men, was let into the castle, and made for the apartments of the favourite. Mortimer was surprised as he sat conferring with the Bishop of Lincoln, and seized before he could offer resistance. But a scuffle ensued, swords were drawn, and two knights were slain before the king's party got the upper hand. The queen burst out of her chamber and threw herself at her son's knees, begging him to "spare her gentle Mortimer", but she was dragged

Edward puts down Mortimer.

---
[1] Afterwards Earl of Salisbury.

away, and the earl was cast into bonds. [October 19, 1330.]

A month later the king called Parliament together, and put the earl on his trial before the peers for murdering Edward II., for overawing the Parliament of Salisbury by armed force, for usurping several royal castles and manors without legal warrant, and for having applied to his own private expenses a large part of the £20,000 paid by the Scots. Without troubling themselves to go through the form of a trial the peers voted that "all the charges contained in the articles of accusation were notoriously true, and that the Earl Marshal should take custody of Roger, Earl of March, and execute him as a traitor and enemy of the king and realm". Accordingly he was hung, drawn, and quartered at Tyburn, on Nov. 29th, 1330. His chief councillor, Sir Simon Bereford, was also condemned and put to death. John Maltravers and Thomas Gurney, the underlings who had actually murdered King Edward II., were not captured: they were proclaimed traitors, and a price set on their heads. Gurney was soon afterwards apprehended in Spain by King Alfonso of Castile and sent homeward in chains; he died on the way, and thus escaped punishment.

The fate of the guilty queen-dowager remained to be settled. After consideration, Edward III. resolved to do no more than relegate his mother to her manor of Castle-Rising, which she was never allowed to quit. She was granted the ample allowance of 3000 marks, and not put in strict confinement. She survived nearly thirty years, and only died in 1358.

Thus all traces of the shameful misgovernment of the years 1327–1330 were swept away. The heirs of the Earl of Kent and other victims of Mortimer were restored to their honours and lands. Pardons were made out for all who had resisted the favourite, and the officials whom he had appointed were obliged to take out fresh grants of their places. A new leaf in the history of the nation was turned over, and the young king began to rule as well as to reign.

CHAPTER II.

FROM THE FALL OF MORTIMER TO THE OUTBREAK OF THE STRUGGLE WITH FRANCE. THE SCOTTISH WAR, 1330-1337.

When the sinister figures of Roger Mortimer and Isabella of France disappeared from the scene, England entered on a more honourable and fortunate period of her history. Everything was now in favour of the young king, and it was to be many years before he forfeited the popularity which he had won by avenging his father's murder and freeing the realm from its shameful bondage. Edward was a handsome, courteous, and generous prince, largely gifted with all the outward graces that win men's hearts. He was an accomplished knight, as distinguished in the tournament in his youth as on the battlefield in his riper years. He loved splendour and display, was a mighty builder, a friend of music and the arts, and a patron of literary men. But though he did not show any of his father's weakness, he was deeply tainted with the moral failings of his ancestor Henry III.,—selfishness, and a chronic incapacity to keep his promises or to pay his debts. All through his life he disregarded the noble watchword of his grandfather Edward I.,—PACTUM SERVA, "abide by the plighted word", and displayed an entire want of sensibility of the sanctity of private pledges or public treaties. More than once he proved that he could be cruel when provoked. In his later years he was destined to show signs of failing vigour long before his due time, and fell into the power of favourites, male and female, who pandered to his failings, and made him even more untrue to the kingly ideal than he had been in early life. His worst fault as a practical ruler was his entire incapacity for understanding finance; he loved the stir and glory of battle, and could never be brought to see that war is the most expensive of luxuries, that great armies must be fed and paid as well as put into

Character of Edward III.

the field. If he had possessed a sterner soul he would have grown into a tyrant, but though hot-tempered and domineering he was neither vindictive nor capable of long-planned and long-enduring schemes of oppression. He was selfish and thoughtless rather than malevolent, and his love of a chivalrous reputation often served him in default of a conscience. England has had many worse kings, and from the constitutional point of view she fared not unprosperously under him. His ambition and his thriftlessness were always causing him to apply to his loving subjects for new grants of money, and money was not given him till he paid for it by confirming charters and conceding privileges to his Parliament.

In 1330, however, Edward had not developed the baser sides of his character, and his subjects were well satisfied with him. During the early years of his personal rule the realm was settling down and recovering somewhat of its peace and good governance. In Mortimer's time disorders of all kinds had been rife, ranging up to the worst forms of open murder and private war. We read, for example, how in 1328 Sir Thomas Wyther, meeting his enemy Robert Lord Holland, in Henley Wood, near Windsor, fell upon him, slew him, and cut off his head, which he carried off on his spear. In 1329 William de la Zouche tried to make valid his pretensions to some of the De Clare estates by raising a great band of his retainers and besieging Caerphilly, the strongest and largest castle of South Wales. We hear of heiresses abducted, manors sacked, and blackmail extorted. Such excesses were put down when there was once more a king who ruled, and served as the fountain of justice. The cessation of the Scottish war allowed the much-ravaged northern shires time to recover themselves. Commerce, too, began to revive, though we still hear of many complaints as to the misdoing of French and Flemish pirates on the high seas.

Civil disorders suppressed.

There were, however, two outstanding questions which were destined to lead to trouble at no very distant date. The first was a dispute as to the homage due to the

French crown for the English possessions in Aquitaine. The elder branch of the old royal house of France had lately died out in the male line (1328), and Philip of Valois, the representative of a younger stock, now reigned at Paris. Edward was, through his mother, descended from the elder line, and seems from the first to have had some notion of refusing to acknowledge Philip as the rightful tenant of the throne. But he had for the time laid the idea aside, and twice did homage to the new king for his Duchy of Aquitaine and County of Ponthieu.[1] Philip, however, was not satisfied with the terms on which homage had been done to him. He proved a bad neighbour, encroached on border lands, encouraged the Gascon barons to make appeals to Paris, and refused to surrender the county of Agenois, which had been seized from Edward II. a few years before. It seems that he had in his mind the expulsion of the English from Southern France, and was biding his time for putting the scheme into operation. For the present nothing but small bickerings along the frontier resulted from his ill-will.

A dispute with Scotland was destined to lead to troubles at a much earlier date, and ultimately to involve King Edward in a war with France also. Its origin lay in one of the clauses of the "Shameful Peace" of Northampton. Robert I. had promised to give back their lands to the unfortunate barons of the English party in Scotland, who had adhered to Edward II. even after Bannockburn, and had been entirely driven out of the realm. But the Bruce died in 1329, and the regents who ruled for his young son David II. proved unable or unwilling to carry out this clause of the treaty. The estates had been, for the most part, seized by or granted out to barons of the nationalist party, who had no intention of surrendering them to their previous owners, whom they regarded as traitors and enemies of their own country. Accordingly the "Disinherited", as

<small>Scotland: the Disinherited Lords.</small>

[1] Ponthieu, a small county at the mouth of the Somme, had come to Edward II. through his mother Eleanor of Castile, whose mother, Joanna, Queen of Castile, had been Countess of Ponthieu in her own right. But the district had been intermittently overrun and occupied by the French.

the exiles were called, found themselves excluded from the promised lands, and wandered disconsolately about England. The chief of them were Gilbert Umphraville, Earl of Angus, David of Strathbogie, Earl of Athole, Walter Comyn, and Henry Lord Beaumont, an English baron who had married the heiress of the great earldom of Buchan. Finding themselves permanently deprived of their rights, these nobles plotted to restore themselves by force of arms, and sent to France for Edward Balliol, the son of the unfortunate John Balliol, who had been king of Scotland in 1292-96. He, like them, had much to recover; not only had he a plausible claim to the Scottish crown, but he regretted the broad Balliol lands in Galloway which his father had lost. Scotland was known to be divided into factions, and ill-ruled by the boy-king's representatives: by a bold and sudden stroke the "Disinherited" hoped to place Balliol on the throne, and win back their old baronies and earldoms. Balliol and his friends, therefore, began secretly to muster their adherents, and to raise mercenary troops. Their action came to King Edward's ears, and he, very properly, refused to allow them to cross the border, and sent orders to his Wardens of the Marches to resist them even by force of arms if they should try to cross the Tweed. Turned back from the land-route, the adventurers hired ships and embarked at Ravenspur, on the Humber, with a little army of 500 men-at-arms and 2000 foot. The rank and file were nearly all English-born, and mainly consisted of archers.

The "Disinherited" landed at Kinghorn, in Fife, and marched on Perth; on their way they were met at the passage of the Earn by the regent, Donald Earl of Mar, with an army at least five times the strength of their own small force. Nevertheless they won a surprising victory. Crossing the river by night, they attacked the Scottish camp. The regent came up against them with his host arranged in three heavy columns of pikemen, such as Wallace had led at Falkirk and Bruce at Bannockburn. The invaders ranged themselves on the hillside of Dupplin

Muir, with the men-at-arms dismounted in a solid clump in the centre, and the archers in a thin semicircular line on the flanks. The Scots climbed the hill and attacked the mailed men who stood beneath Balliol's banner, neglecting the bowmen as unworthy of their notice. But while they were pushing the men-at-arms uphill by force of numbers, the arrow-shower beat so fiercely upon their flanks that they were finally brought to a standstill. The slaughter in the side columns was so great that they fell in upon the main column in disorder and stopped its advance. Every moment that they stood halted, brought new losses from the pitiless rain of shafts, and at last the great mass broke up and rolled down the hill in rout. The "Disinherited" mounted their horses to pursue, and made a cruel slaughter of the fugitives. Among the slain were the regent, Donald of Mar, three earls, and seventy knights, besides many thousands of foot-soldiers. *[margin: Battle of Dupplin Muir.]*

The blow inflicted by the defeat of Dupplin was so heavy that Balliol had no difficulty in seizing Perth and Stirling, and getting himself crowned at Scone as king of Scotland, while the young David Bruce fled overseas to France and took refuge with King Philip. Balliol at once wrote to Edward III. announcing that he had won back his realm, and was prepared to hold it as a fief of the English crown as his ancestors had been wont to do. He offered, as an extra inducement to secure King Edward's support, to surrender the important and much-disputed frontier post of Berwick.

The English monarch had summoned his Parliament to discuss the acceptance of these terms, when news came which put a new face upon affairs. Balliol had lost his realm as quickly as he had gained it. Though a good soldier he was not himself a man of much mark or influence, and his followers, the Disinherited Lords, had upset all the internal arrangements of Scotland by violently taking possession of their lost estates. The Bruce's party took advantage of the general unrest and discontent to form a conspiracy. As Balliol lay at Annan, *[margin: Balliol driven out.]*

near Dumfries, with but a small guard around him, he was suddenly attacked by John Earl of Murray, and Sir Archibald Douglas. They fell upon him at midnight, scattered or slew his retainers, and chased him to the gates of Carlisle. [Dec. 16, 1332.] Immediately risings set in all over Scotland, and the new king's followers were hunted out of the country. Archibald Douglas was installed as regent for the absent David II., and his authority was everywhere recognized. Plundering parties of Scottish moss-troopers soon began to cross the Cheviots and resumed the raids of the days of Robert Bruce.

Edward III. had now to choose between David II. and Balliol. He was young, enterprising, and ambitious, and much set on avenging the discomfiture he had suffered during the campaign of 1327. Accordingly he resolved to recognize Balliol as king, to accept his homage and the cession of Berwick, and to restore him to the Scottish throne by force of arms. The recent raids into Northumberland supplied him with a plausible *casus belli*.

Accordingly in March 1333 he gathered a great army and marched for the border. Balliol and his friends the "Disinherited" joined him with their retainers, and siege was laid to Berwick. For ten weeks the strong harbour-town held out, but at last food grew scarce within the walls, and the garrison offered to surrender if not relieved by the month of July, and gave hostages for the performance of their promise. Before the appointed day a small body of troops under Sir William Keith slipped between the besiegers' lines and succeeded in entering the place, though they could do nothing to drive off the English. They brought news, however, that the regent was at hand with the whole armed force of Scotland at his back. The governor held that Keith's appearance relieved him from his obligation to open the gates, and held out when the fixed period had elapsed. The English king saw the matter otherwise, and when entrance was still refused him, cruelly hung the hostages in front of the castle gate.

Siege of Berwick.

Some ten days later the army of succour came in sight.

Douglas had brought with him a formidable army of 30,000 men, and the English were forced to choose whether they would fight or raise the siege. Edward left part of his army in his lines, to blockade the town, and took post with the rest on Halidon Hill, a rising ground three miles north of Berwick, which commands the road from Dunbar and Edinburgh. It was a good position, with a marshy bottom before it and a line of wood along its brow. The king drew up his army in three corps at the head of the slope: he himself took the centre, his brother, John of Eltham, the right, Edward Balliol the left. In each division the men-at-arms sent their horses away and stood on foot in a solid body in the middle, while two wings of archers stretched out on each flank of them. This was the same array that the "Disinherited" had used at Dupplin, and we cannot doubt that the English king chose it on the advice of Balliol and his friends, the victors in the earlier fight.

This order of battle proved as effective on the second occasion as on the first. The Scots were forced to attack, under pain of seeing Berwick succumb in a few days: accordingly the regent formed his host in three heavy columns, just as Donald of Mar had done at Dupplin, and launched them against the English position. They were much delayed by the marsh, but waded through it and began to ascend the opposite slope. But the arrow-shower beat so fiercely upon them that it took them a long time to climb the hill, each party that forced its way to the head of the column being shot down ere it could close. Only at one or two points did the Scots succeed in reaching the brow, and getting to hand-strokes with the English men-at-arms. They were repelled on each occasion, for their order was lost, and the main body never reached the battle-front. At last they recoiled back to the marsh, the English following them and making great slaughter of the fugitives. The regent was slain, as were also the Earls of Carrick, Menteith, Lennox, Strathern, and Sutherland, with ten thousand of their followers. This disaster came upon

Battle of Halidon Hill.

them because they had neglected the wise precepts of Robert Bruce, and attacked a strong position well lined with archers, to whose missiles they had nothing to oppose. [July 19, 1333.]

Berwick surrendered next day, and since no Scottish army was any longer in the field, Edward was able to march into the Lowlands unopposed, and replaced his dependant Balliol on the throne. A permanent pacification might perhaps have followed but for the English king's greed: he bade Balliol sign a treaty ceding to him not only Berwick but all the Border shires of Scotland as far as Edinburgh.[1] The Scots could not tolerate the partition of their realm, and rose again to drive out their new master. Balliol had to fly to Berwick and seek English aid once more; it was given him with an unsparing hand, and he was twice able to reconquer the whole land as far as Perth. [1334-1335.]

Balliol was still maintaining a precarious hold upon the Scottish crown, when a new series of complications began to arise, which were destined to draw English attention away from the Scottish war. Philip of France had never ceased to give trouble on the frontier of the English possessions in Aquitaine. He now began to send aid, at first with some pretence of secrecy, but soon with perfect openness, to the patriotic party in Scotland. French men-at-arms crossed the North Sea to fight against Balliol, and French privateers cruised along the eastern coast of England, capturing merchant vessels and gradually making trade impossible. David Bruce dwelt at the court of Paris, and sent his partisans in the North promises of continued aid from his ally. At last rumours reached King Edward that considerable squadrons were being prepared at Calais and in the Norman ports for an actual invasion of England. Credibility was lent to the report by piratical raids made by parties of French in Jersey, Guernsey, and the Isle of Wight. It was obvious that if Edward continued to bestow all

Troubles with France.

---

[1] Viz., the three Lothians, Berwick, Roxburgh, Peebles, Selkirk, and Dumfries.

his attention on Scotland he might ere long find himself attacked in the rear. [1336.]

Accordingly Edward set to work to face the prospect of war with France, and began to send ambassadors to the Emperor Lewis of Bavaria and the princes of the Netherlands, to secure alliances with them against King Philip. By the promise of great subsidies he bought the aid of the Dukes of Brabant and Guelders and the Counts of Holland and Hainault. He also negotiated a league with the Flemish cities, who were greatly discontented with their ruler, Louis Count of Flanders, a devoted vassal and supporter of the French king. The Flemings had no wish to make war on England, with which they transacted an immense trade, buying the fine English wool and making it into cloth, which they sold all over Northern Europe. When Count Louis seized and imprisoned all the English merchants he could lay hands on (Oct. 1336), his subjects were so enraged with him for stirring up war, that they entered into correspondence with King Edward, and offered to aid him even against their own feudal lord. The lead in the rising was taken by Jacob van Artevelde, the famous brewer of Ghent, a wealthy citizen who had turned demagogue, and ruled the guilds of his native town with a despotic sway by means of his ready tongue and his strong will. The count's power in Flanders was small compared with that of his turbulent subject.

Emboldened by the knowledge that he would not lack allies on the Continent, Edward began to treat the French king much as Philip had been treating him for the last four years. He gave shelter to Robert Count of Artois, a French prince of the royal house who had been driven into exile by his cousin, and began to gather together a fleet in order to pay back the late piratical raids on the English coast. In October, 1337, he made war inevitable by laying formal claim to the crown of France, and denouncing Philip as a usurper. It is said that he took this step at the instigation of the Flemings, who told him that they had sworn allegiance to the King of France, and that if he assumed the title it would of course be due to him and not to the representative of the line of Valois.

Edward's claim was a very poor one. He represented that his mother was sister to Charles IV., the last king of the elder line, and that he therefore should have succeeded

THE FRENCH SUCCESSION.

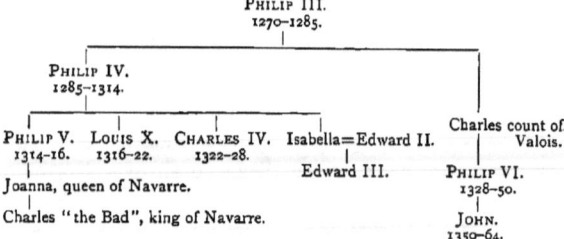

to the throne in 1328 rather than Philip, who was but cousin to King Charles. But there was no instance in French history of right to the crown being transmitted by a female, and the peers of France had ruled that the nearest male heir should succeed. There being no precedent to guide them, they based their decision on a text in the Salic Law, a code of the ancient Franks, which laid down that landed property should go to the male representative of the house. The case had never before arisen in France, for since the house of Capet came to the throne in the 10th century every king had left sons behind him. Undoubtedly the French had the best right to decide who should reign over them, and their voice had unanimously been given in favour of Philip. Edward had practically surrendered his claim when in 1329 he had done homage to his cousin for the duchy of Aquitaine; it was absurd to exhume it eight years later. Moreover, even if it were granted that rights might pass through a female, his case was a bad one. For his mother's brothers had daughters whose title was better than that of their aunt. On Ed-

Edward's claim to the French crown.

ward's principles the rightful king of France should have been Charles of Navarre, the son of the daughter of Philip V., his mother's eldest brother. [See table on page 24.]

The claim now asserted was to have the most disastrous results, involving England in a lingering war, whose last blow was not struck till 1453. The vain name of King of France was not surrendered even when the last scrap of territory across the Channel was lost, and continued to be appended to the formal title of the English kings down to the reign of George III.

The commencement of the "Hundred Years' War" had perhaps been rendered inevitable by Philip's persistent intrigues and encroachments. But it was an ill day for England when King Edward formulated his claims to his cousin's crown, and so embittered the strife. The nation had been rapidly recovering from the effects of the reign of Edward II., but it still needed peace and rest. The Scottish war had not much tried its resources, but the bloody and expensive struggle which began in 1337 was to prove a far more serious drain upon its resources. In his reckless and thriftless management of it King Edward was destined to develop all the faults of his character, which had hitherto been hidden from his subjects, who, since Halidon Hill, had worshipped him as the avenger of Bannockburn and the best knight in Christendom.

CHAPTER III.

THE FIRST STAGE OF THE HUNDRED YEARS' WAR, 1337–1349. FROM THE OUTBREAK OF WAR TO THE BLACK DEATH.

In the autumn of 1337 the long bickering between England and France, which had hitherto been confined to piratical incursions and unauthorized raids, ended in open war. The Earl of Derby, son of Henry Earl of

Lancaster, was sent over to Flanders to raise the king's
War in Flanders. Netherlandish allies. He came ashore on the isle of Cadzand, where he found the troops of the Flemish count prepared to oppose him, though the majority of the people of the land welcomed the advent of the invaders. Derby beat off the count's men-at-arms with ease, for they could make no head against the English archers; they fled in all directions, leaving their leader Guy, the count's bastard brother, a prisoner in the earl's hands. [Oct. 1337.]

Edward himself was not able to follow so soon as he had hoped, for he found himself unable easily to collect the money needed for raising a large army. Parliament granted him the means of procuring a great sum by the expedient of permitting him to buy 20,000 sacks of wool at £3 a sack from the wool-growers, and to sell it abroad at the best profit that he could make, while other exporters of the commodity, if natives, were to be taxed forty shillings a sack, and if foreigners sixty shillings. In addition, the barons and knights gave him a tax of "a fifteenth", and the town and clergy one of "a tenth" on their property.[1] These liberal votes were to prove quite insufficient for the king's thriftless hand. Edward sailed in July, 1338, from Orwell with 1600 men-at-arms and 10,000 archers, but their maintenance was only a small part of his expenses. He took into his pay all the princes of the Netherlands, who were far more anxious to get the English money than to set their troops in the field. He also went to Coblenz and wasted vast sums in a magnificent conference with the emperor, Lewis the Bavarian, who granted him in return for cash the empty title of Vicar-general of the Empire for the parts west of the Rhine. Edward soon found that this dignity gave him no more power than he had before, and he had the greatest difficulty in inducing the Duke of Brabant and his other allies to join him with their vassals. He could not get them mustered till the spring of the following year; mean-

[1] The latter grants were made by the Parliament of Sept.–Oct. 1337, the former by that of February, 1338.

while he, with his court and his army, lay at Antwerp spending much money to no profit.

The king's enforced idleness seemed all the more exasperating when news came that King Philip had gathered a great fleet of Norman and Picard ships, strengthened by a squadron hired from the Genoese, and had sent them forth to ravage the south coast of England. They landed at Southampton "on a Sunday when all the people were at mass", and sacked and burned the place. Next they passed on to Portsmouth and did the like with it and the neighbouring villages. Then they returned to France with their plunder quite unmolested. This expedition deserves memory for the fact that the French fleet carried the first cannon which the English had ever seen; they were little pieces described as "iron pots throwing iron bolts by the force of gunpowder", and did nothing effective. But their appearance marks the first beginnings of a new stage in the art of war. [Late autumn of 1338.] *The French ravage the South Coast.*

In the following summer King Edward at last got his refractory allies together, and marched into France with an army which is said to have amounted to nearly 100,000 men. But this great host effected nothing; they laid siege to Cambray, but failed to take it, and then marched through the Cambrésis and Vermandois ravaging the land. King Philip came out against them with an army as large as their own, but he acted most cautiously, posting himself behind woods and marshes, where he could not easily be assailed. It was to no purpose that Edward drew up his army and offered battle more than once; the French would not leave their position and could not be attacked in it. At last, when his provisions were exhausted and his foreign allies began to steal home, Edward was forced to retire ingloriously into Brabant, having accomplished absolutely nothing by his mighty display of force. *Edward invades France.*

Meanwhile all the parliamentary grants were spent, and the king found himself in dire poverty. He wrote urgently to ask for more money, for he was already £30,000 in debt, though he had had the handling of £300,000, a sum which seemed almost incredible to the men of the fourteenth century. He had even pawned his crown of state to the Archbishop of Trier for 60,000 florins. He was forced to come home to raise more funds in the spring of 1340, and obtained the very liberal grant from parliament of "the ninth lamb, the ninth fleece, and the ninth sheaf for the two years next to come". But this was not conceded to him without conditions; he was made to swear to redress many grievances, such as the extortions of his sheriffs and purveyors. Moreover, he was made to promise never again to raise a "tallage", *i.e.* an arbitrary tax on the towns and manors which lay in the royal demesne.

Having once more some money in his purse, Edward resolved to set out again for Flanders. But he received news, which turned out to be quite correct, that the French fleet which had ravaged the south coast in the previous year was again at sea, and intended to intercept his passage. It was necessary at all costs to gain command of the narrow seas, and all the ports of England were ordered to equip vessels and send them to the harbour of Orwell, in Suffolk, from which the king was to sail. On June 22nd 1340, nearly 200 ships, small and great, weighed anchor for Flanders. The French were not met on the open water, but when the Flemish coast drew near it was seen that a perfect forest of masts lay in the port of Sluys. The enemy was waiting there with a fleet about the same in number as that of King Edward —it was said there were 190 sail—but 19 of them were "so great that the like of them had never before been seen". These appear to have been the Genoese vessels, which were true ships of war, and not mere armed merchantmen like the rest of the two fleets.

The enemy was moored in three lines, with ship laid close to ship and barricades built across them, so that it was impossible to force a passage between them. But Edward, by feigning to fly, induced them to cast off and pursue him. He then turned

Battle of Sluys.

and plunged in among the hostile ships. The battle was a confused medley without any manœuvring, for the fleets lay wedged together broadside to broadside, and most of the work was done by boarding. The English archers gradually shot down the hostile crossbowmen, who could not stand firm against them for long. Then the knights clambered from ship to ship and swept the decks of the enemy. Edward himself was in the thickest of the fight, and won the admiration of all men by his audacious courage. By the afternoon the French fleet was completely crushed, two-thirds of the ships were captured, and more than 20,000 men were drowned or slain. This great fight, the second naval victory in the English annals, put an end to any attempt of the French to dispute the dominion of the seas. For the rest of the war the English went where they would, and always made the sea their base of attack. [24th June, 1340.]

But splendid as was the victory of Sluys, it had but a negative effect on the general fortune of the war. It prevented any chance of the invasion of England by the French, but it did not give King Edward any help in prosecuting his plans for overrunning Northern France at the head of his Netherlandish allies. Soon after his arrival in Flanders he mustered them, and led them to besiege Tournay. [July, 1340.] But he found himself as wholly unable to take the place as he had been to reduce Cambray in his last expedition. After lying before it for two months, he found that his cash was all spent, and that his allies were melting away from him. Meanwhile King Philip had appeared at the head of a large army, and was watching the leaguer from a distance, though he utterly refused to offer any opportunity for a battle. *Second fruitless campaign in France.* Edward found that he could do nothing; the rains of autumn were beginning, no more money came in from England, and vexatious news had arrived that the French were winning castle after castle on the borders of Aquitaine, and that the Scots had once more driven out Edward Balliol, and sent their plundering bands across the Tweed. Depressed in spirits, and conscious of his helplessness, the king stooped to propose a truce to his enemy. Philip, who had secret intelligence that Tournay was suffering terribly from famine and might surrender at any moment, gladly listened to the offer, and an armistice, to last for nine months, and to extend to Scotland and Aquitaine, was signed. [Sep., 1340.] Edward promptly disbanded his army, and returned to England in great wrath, blaming every one rather than himself for the failure of his campaign.

The moment that he reached London the king gave vent to his wrath by the wholesale dismissal or arrest of his ministers, whom he unjustly accused of having wrecked his plan of campaign by embezzling or dissipating the money which Parliament had voted him. He deprived his chancellor, Robert Stratford, Bishop of Chichester, of the seals, put the treasurer, Northburgh Bishop of Lichfield, in custody, and imprisoned Stonor, the chief justice, with some of his colleagues, the chief clerk of the chancery, the mayor of London, and many more. But Archbishop Stratford (the chancellor's brother) bore the brunt of his wrath; having been practically acting as prime minister for some years, he was the person on whom Edward laid most of the blame. It was attempted to bring him to trial for maladministration, but he claimed the right to be judged only by "his peers", the barons and bishops of the House of Lords. Stratford met with general support, and Edward was compelled to yield when a committee of the Lords reported in favour of the archbishop's contention, and laid down the doctrine that "peers cannot be arrested, judged, or outlawed save in full Parliament before their peers". The king's wrath soon burned out, and he acknowledged himself to be in the wrong by reconciling himself to Stratford, releasing his prisoners, and humbly suing Parliament for fresh supplies. These were only granted him after he had conceded three very important constitutional privileges. The first was that he should recognize the right of the peers which had just been asserted by the archbishop, the second that his ministers should in future be appointed in Parliament, and

Edward's quarrel with Stratford.

sworn to obey all the laws of the realm, and the third that Parliament should appoint commissioners to audit all the accounts of money voted for the king's service. Thus the Lords and Commons obtained two most important means of checking the king's rash actions: they were to have a hand in the appointing of his ministers and in the auditing of his revenues. [May, 1341.] But Edward had the shameful duplicity to make a private protest that he did not hold himself bound by his word, and some months later openly declared that "he had dissembled, as he was justified in doing, in allowing the pretended statute to be sealed for that time, for all acts done in prejudice of his royal prerogative were null and void". [Oct., 1341.] *Edward's treachery to Parliament.*

For two years after this scandalous trick Edward did not dare to call a Parliament. Meanwhile the war languished, mainly for want of money, but also because the Emperor Lewis and most of the other useless allies of England dropped away and made separate truces with France. On the Scottish border things went from bad to worse; Stirling and Edinburgh fell into the hands of the patriots in 1341, and Balliol's hold on his uneasy throne was so completely lost that he had to take up his permanent residence in England.

It would now have been best to make peace with both France and Scotland, and acknowledge that the war was a failure. But Edward's energies were not yet exhausted, and he was just about to be presented with a new opportunity of vexing King Philip. A bitter war of succession broke out in Brittany, the second most important fief of the French crown; its cause had some similarity to the dispute which was already raging between Philip and Edward for the crown of France. When Duke John III. died in 1341 the duchy was claimed both by his eldest brother's daughter, Jeanne Countess of Blois, as nearest of kin, and by his younger brother, John of Montfort, as nearest heir male. There was some irony in the fact that King Philip, whose crown had come to him as heir male of Charles IV., supported the *Civil War in Brittany.*

Countess of Blois, while Edward, whose French claim rested on the theory that rights could be transmitted by a female, became the advocate of Montfort, who was urging the doctrine of the Salic Law.[1]

At first the party of the countess had the best of the civil war in Brittany. Aided by French troops they took Nantes, the capital of the duchy, and made prisoner John of Montfort, who had shut himself up within its walls. But the courageous Jeanne de Nevers, Montfort's wife, maintained the cause of her captive spouse, and held out in the strong castle of Hennebont till she was relieved by the arrival of English troops under Sir Walter Manny, a great mercenary captain from Hainault, who was one of the most trusted officers of King Edward. Shortly afterwards the king himself arrived with a considerable army, and cleared Western Brittany of the French and the partisans of Blois. But he failed to take Nantes and Rennes, and all the eastern parts of the duchy remained in the hands of the enemy. [1342.]

The campaign had been a success for neither party, and was ended by a truce which might have turned into a peace but for the inveterate personal hostility between Philip and Edward. [Jan., 1343.] It was difficult, too, to come to a satisfactory conclusion about the Breton matter, as neither claimant had got possession of the whole duchy. Philip, contrary to his agreement, kept Montfort in prison till he escaped in 1345 and got back to Hennebont. But the truce lasted

Truce for three years.

---

[1] THE BRETON SUCCESSION.

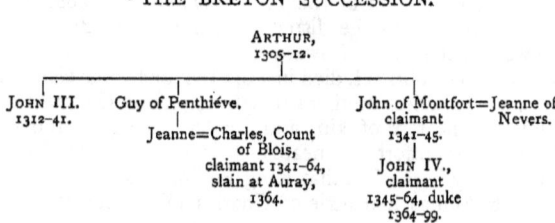

for three years, though border fighting never wholly ceased either in Brittany or in Aquitaine.

In 1343 Edward had again called a Parliament, which confirmed the truce, and advised him to make a peace also, if good terms could be obtained, or, if not, to make open war. But the unsatisfactory suspension of hostilities was all that could be gained. Meanwhile the national council engaged in a sharp dispute with the pope, a matter in which they had for once their master's full sympathy. The pope was now dwelling at Avignon, whither Clement V. had migrated in 1310, and was wholly under the influence and domination of the French king. The main subject of grievance against him was his inordinate greed in appointing "Provisors" to English sees and benefices. He kept nominating foreigners to rich preferments whenever they fell vacant, in utter disregard of the rights of the king and other patrons. The clerics so named drew their revenues, but seldom or never came near their cures, to the great injury of the church. As the English complaint ran, Clement VI. "appointed foreigners, most of them scandalous persons, who do not reside on their benefices, nor know the faces of the flocks intrusted to them, who do not understand their speech, but neglecting the cure of souls, seek, as hirelings, only temporal lucre. The Successor of the Apostles was surely appointed to feed and not to shear the Lord's sheep." The king had the full approval of the nation when, in 1344, he issued a mandate forbidding any person to bring Papal bulls or any such documents into England except by his leave. This was a reassertion of an old prohibition: as long ago as the eleventh century William the Conqueror had published a similar edict; but now it needed to be once more clearly set forth. It was not, however, till 1352 that Parliament passed the "Statute of Provisors", which rendered liable to arrest and imprisonment all clerics who endeavoured to make use of Papal documents contrary to the interest of the king and the realm.

Quarrels with the Papacy.

By the end of 1345 it was quite clear that no permanent

peace with France could be procured, and the king resolved to recommence the series of invasions which had hitherto been so fruitless. This time he did not make the Netherlands his base; his allies in that direction had proved faithless, and his chief supporter, Jacob van Artevelde, had lately been murdered in a riot. Though the Flemish towns still continued attached to England, nearly all the neighbouring states had made agreements with King Philip. Nor was Brittany chosen as the starting-point of the attack: Edward had determined to aim at the heart of France, by landing in Normandy and striking at Paris. He sent Henry of Lancaster, Earl of Derby, with a small army to defend Aquitaine, but reserved the main force for his own command. Derby, it may be mentioned, proved as good a soldier in Guyenne as he had already shown himself at the battle of Cadzand, and gave the enemy a sound beating at Auberoche (Oct. 23, 1345). He drew down to the south a great French army under Philip's son John, which was still engaged in operations on the Garonne when Edward made his great assault on the lands around the Seine.

Edward invades Normandy.

On July 11, 1346, the king landed at Cape La Hogue with an army entirely composed of native English, and therefore much smaller than the host of Confederates which had taken the field in Flanders in 1338 and 1341. It included about 4000 men-at-arms, 12,000 English archers, 6000 Welsh light troops, and also a small contingent of Irish. The landing in Normandy was quite unexpected: Edward had concealed his purpose, and everyone had thought that the army was intended to aid the Earl of Derby in Guyenne. The French were wholly unprepared for an assault in this quarter, and Edward was able to march through Normandy for many days without meeting with much opposition; he ravaged the countryside and took several open towns—Barfleur, Valognes, Carentan, and St. Lo, one after the other. At Caen he first met with a hostile force, but easily routed the Norman militia, and took prisoner their leaders, the

Counts of Tancarville and Eu, the Chamberlain and Constable of France. After plundering the rich town he struck at Rouen, but could not reach it, for the French had broken all the bridges of the lower Seine. Then Edward turned his invasion into a hazardous adventure: he sent his fleet home to England loaded with the spoils of Normandy, and marched on Paris, keeping south of the Seine. This was a dangerous move, for the French had now begun to assemble in great force, and since Edward had not fortified for himself any post in Normandy, he had no place of refuge or friendly territory nearer than Guyenne or Flanders on to which he could retire. Paris was far too strong to be taken by a sudden attack, and this was so self-evident that it seems probable that the English king was merely carrying out a chivalrous adventure when he marched to beard King Philip in his capital. No opposition of importance was met with on the way, but when the invaders drew near the southern gates of Paris they heard that King Philip had collected 60,000 men or more at St. Denis, and had even been joined by part of his son's army from Guyenne. The leisurely pace at which Edward had crossed Normandy had permitted his rival to concentrate all his forces. It was impossible to go on, and the English had to choose between a march on Bordeaux and one on Flanders. Nor was the latter alternative easy to take, for the Seine had first to be crossed, and all its bridges were broken. It was nevertheless this choice which Edward determined to make: he hastily moved on the broken bridge of Poissy, ten miles below Paris, and drove off its guards by the force of his archery. Then the army hastily repaired the ruined arches with planks, and succeeded in crossing before King Philip and his host could come up.

The march on Paris.

Edward now hurried north with all speed, the French king following as hastily a day's march in his rear. They kept their distance till the English vanguard reached the Somme: here Edward found all the bridges broken, and the militia of Picardy drawn up to oppose him on the further side. He made three attempts to cross at various points near Amiens, but was foiled in every one. Meanwhile the pursuers were in close contact with his rear, and it seemed that he might be caught between the French army and the peat-bogs of the impassable Somme. Things were looking desperate when a peasant pointed out to the king a dangerous ford, named Blanchetaque, the lowest on the river's course, below Abbeville and near the sea. Here the stream was tidal, and at low water the ford was open for four hours at a time. A body of Picard levies was waiting on the further bank, and the passage was deep, but there was no other chance of saving the army, so the king bade his men-at-arms enter the water and force their way over. Meanwhile the archers kept up a long-range fire across the stream to gall the militia on the opposite bank. After hard fighting the English horsemen drove off the Picards, and the whole army waded after them across the Somme. King Philip came up just in time to find the tide rising and the river once more impassable.

Passage of the Somme.

Edward had thus gained a day's start of the pursuers, and had the open road to Flanders before him He marched on as far as the village of Crecy, and then unexpectedly bade his army halt and announced his intention of offering battle. "He was now in his own rightful inheritance, the county of Ponthieu, and was ready to fight and to take what fortune God should send him." The fact was that he had found an admirable position in front of Crecy, and that, even if beaten, he had a safe retreat on Flanders.

The host was drawn up on the hillside just east of Crecy, its right flank covered by the brook of the Maye and by a thick forest, while its left rested on the orchards of the village of Wadicourt. There was a valley in front, beyond which lay the rising ground over which the French army would appear. The English were arrayed in three corps, two in the front line, the third in reserve. The southern wing was put nominally under the charge of the young Edward Prince of Wales, a lad of sixteen now taking his first sight of war: he was placed under the care of the Earls of Warwick and Oxford, two experienced soldiers. The northern or left wing was under the Earls of Northampton and Arundel. The king himself stood behind, at the top of the hill, with the reserve corps. In each division the men-at-arms had sent their horses to the rear, and stood on foot in a solid mass, after the manner of Dupplin and Halidon. The archers formed wings, thrown out on each side of the central

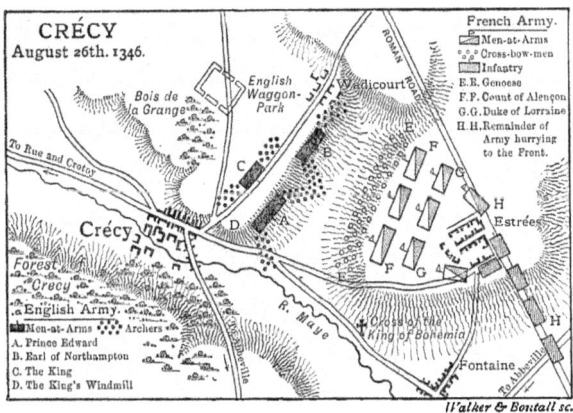

clumps of spears, and leaning forward on the flanks so as to partly encircle an enemy who should charge directly at the men-at-arms.

King Philip had marched from Abbeville under the impression that the English were in full flight for Flanders. Hence it was no small surprise to him to find them drawn up in line of battle on the hill by Crecy. His army was strung out over many miles of road, and the rear was only just setting out from Abbeville when the van was already almost in contact with the English. At first he came to the wise resolve to defer the battle till the next day, but the fiery barons in the front refused to halt, and pushed in so close to the hostile position that fighting became inevitable. Forced by his vassals' want of discipline to attack before he had intended, Philip drew up his army as best he could. His front line was formed by 6000 crossbowmen, mainly Genoese mercenaries, who were bidden to drive back the English archers Behind them rode a great mass of men-at-arms under the Counts of Alençon and Flanders: the other contingents were gradually coming up and taking ground to the rear in successive lines.

The Genoese marched up to the foot of the English slope, and began to let fly, but the moment that they started the engagement the archers "took one step forward, drew the arrows back to the ear, and shot so fast and so thick that it seemed as if it were snowing". Their aim was accurate, and their discharge five or six times as rapid as that of the clumsy crossbow, which required to be wound up after every discharge. In a few minutes the Genoese were hopelessly routed, and fled back towards their own main body. The Count of Alençon, who had no experience of the English archery, cursed them for cowards, and in his rage bade his men-at-arms ride over them, and make straight for the enemy's front. This act was as mad as it was cruel. The horsemen trod down many of the wretched infantry, but were hampered by the crowd, and could only push through in small broken parties toward the English. When they came in range they soon found that they had erred in despising their enemy: the archers shot down well-nigh every one who came near them. Only a very few of the French got to close quarters, and charged in on the dismounted knights of the Prince of Wales and the Earl of Northampton: Alençon and Lewis of Flanders were both slain. Angered, but not cowed, by this unfortunate opening of the battle, King Philip launched each of his corps as it reached the field against the English line: all had the same fate as the first-comers. But the French noblesse was brave and obstinate, and their fruitless attacks did not cease till nightfall. Only once did a

Battle of Crecy.

large body succeed in closing with the Prince of Wales's corps. King Edward was asked for succour, but refused to bid the reserve charge, observing that "the boy must win his spurs". His action was justified, for the French were beaten off without it being necessary to engage the rear division.

At dusk the French fell into hopeless disorder, and melted away from the field. Edward would not allow any pursuit lest his little army might get broken up in the dark. Next morning the extent of the victory could be gauged: there lay dead in front of the English line at least ten thousand men, of whom no less than 1552 were counts, barons, and knights. The most notable among the dead was John King of Bohemia, an ally of France, who, though he was almost blind, had insisted on leading a charge at the head of the knights of his household. He and they were found all dead together in front of the Prince of Wales's standard. The Duke of Lorraine and ten counts were slain, with half the baronage of Northern France.

Such was the result of the rash attempt of the French chivalry to ride down the dismounted men-at-arms of King Edward, flanked by the deadly archery of the English yeomanry. So complete was the victory that Edward could now choose his own course of action without fear of being further molested. He resolved to besiege and take Calais, the great French port which faces Dover across the narrow strait. If taken it would give England an open door into France: moreover, the English had an old grudge against its seamen, who were noted privateers and pirates, and had often ravaged Kent and Sussex.

While Edward lay before Calais news reached him of a second victory almost as important as that which he had himself won. King David of Scotland had taken advantage of the absence of the English host to invade the northern counties. The Scots, we are told, "thought that no one was left in England save millers and mass-priests", and hoped to find the border ill-guarded. They

40   ENGLAND AND THE HUNDRED YEARS' WAR.

forced their way nearly as far as Durham, till they were met at Neville's Cross by the militia of the northern coun-
<small>Battle of Neville's Cross.</small> ties, headed by the Lords Percy and Neville and by Edward Balliol, their former sovereign, who had now practically relapsed into the condition of an English baron.[1] Here King David suffered a sanguinary defeat; once more the archers were too much for the Scottish pikemen, and the tragedy of Halidon Hill was repeated (Oct. 17th, 1346). David himself was taken prisoner, with many of his nobles, and was retained in captivity for ten years. He was not unkindly treated, but one of his companions, John Earl of Menteith, a former partisan of Balliol who had betrayed his master and was specially obnoxious to the English, was beheaded as a traitor—a piece of illogical and unnecessary cruelty, since half the Scottish nobility might have fallen under the same accusation.

After Crecy King Edward's arms were successful in all directions. The Earl of Derby (now become Earl of Lancaster by his father's death) thrust the French out of Aquitaine; Sir Thomas Dagworth, placed in command in Brittany, routed the partisans of Charles of Blois at Roche
<small>Capture of Calais.</small> Darien, and in the north the siege of Calais went steadily on. King Philip collected an army, and came up to endeavour to raise the léaguer, but with the memory of Crecy before him he dared not attack the English lines, and after his departure the place was starved out and yielded on terms (Aug. 3, 1347).[2]

King Edward permitted those of the burghers who would do him homage to retain their houses, but drove out the large majority who preferred to abide by their French allegiance. Their place was filled up by the immigration of several thousand English merchants and

---

[1] He was lord of Barnard Castle and other North Country estates.

[2] The story that Edward intended to hang seven of the burgesses, who offered themselves as victims in behalf of the whole town, and that they were only spared at Queen Philippa's intercession, seems an invention. But the leaders "surrendered themselves to the king's mercy", and came out barefoot and with halters round their necks, as a sign that they were wholly in his hands to spare or slay. Hence probably the story. Edward made them hostages, but treated them kindly.

seafaring folk, and Calais became for two hundred years a thoroughly English town. On one occasion it even sent members to the Parliament at Westminster. For the future all the inroads of the English into Northern France were sent out from this invaluable "open door". The town also developed into a great centre for trade with Flanders. Repeated attempts of the French to recover it by treachery or by open force all came to nothing.

A short time after the fall of Calais another of the numerous truces which interrupted the course of the Hundred Years' War was concluded, leaving each party to hold what it was actually in possession of at the moment. It would probably have been short, but for a great calamity which fell on both England and France in the following year. In 1347 a deadly pestilence, coming from India and the Euphrates valley, where malignant disorders are always rife, appeared at Constantinople. In the next year it swept over Italy and reached the West: by the summer of 1348 it was raging both in England and France.

The "Black Death", as this plague was generally named, seems to have been a kind of eruptive typhoid fever, highly contagious and breaking forth with boils upon the body. In the crowded insanitary towns of mediæval Europe, among a people utterly ignorant of the simplest laws of health, it spread like wildfire. But the countryside suffered almost as much as the cities. Many districts did not recover for centuries from its effects: the whole Norse population of Greenland died off, so that the very existence of that ancient colony was forgotten. Many depopulated parishes in Sweden relapsed into the forest from which they had been hewn out. The Grand Duke of Moscow and 60,000 of his subjects were cut off: Florence lost 100,000 inhabitants in eight months. England suffered as much as other regions, for a whole year (Aug. 1348–Sep. 1349) she was labouring under the scourge: the coming of the winter cold brought no relief, and it was noted that rainy weather, which was abnormally prevalent that year, seemed

The Black Death.

to be particularly favourable to the spread of the plague. The king's daughter Joanna died of it on the eve of her betrothal to Don Pedro of Castile—a fortunate release for her, as he was a cruel and reckless prince, and actually murdered the French lady, Blanche of Bourbon, whom he wedded in her stead. Two Archbishops of Canterbury fell victims to it, John de Ufford and the scholastic philosopher Thomas Bradwardine, whom men called "the *doctor profundus*". The clergy indeed, owing to their duties at the death-bed, suffered even more than other classes. Some two-thirds of the livings of the diocese of Norwich changed hands during the twelvemonth, as is shown by the bishop's register. In Yorkshire the mortality, though somewhat lower, yet carried off more than a half of the parish priests. Grass grew in the marketplace of Bristol. London buried some 50,000 corpses in the new cemetery, of thirteen acres in extent, which was consecrated on ground belonging to the Hospital of St. Bartholomew in Spitalfields. The cattle strayed through the corn and found none to drive them away. Ships were driven ashore on the coast of the North Sea with all their crews lying dead on board. On the whole, it is probable that there was not much exaggeration in the contemporary estimate which calculated that England lost a full half of her population during the terrible thirteen months during which the Black Death raged. All description of local records, such as manor rolls and the like, seem to bear out the statement.

The social and political results of the Black Death were naturally tremendous and wide-spread. It seems to have generated selfish indifference and demoralization, and its most prominent consequence was the outbreak of a crisis in the relations of the land-owning and the labouring classes. So large a number of the agricultural class had been swept away, that the lords of the manors could not get their lands tilled, for the survivors demanded wages that seemed extortionate to their employers. The latter fell back on their ancient right to demand the unpaid labour of their villeins during

<small>Results of the Black Death.</small>

a certain number of days in every year. This practice had been dropping into disuse for many generations, for the landholders had been commuting forced labour for money, and so allowing their peasants to become rent-paying tenants rather than serfs. The attempt to enforce this half-obsolete practice led to numberless disputes. Many villeins absconded, others formed themselves into secret leagues to resist the lords' claims. It was to no purpose that Parliament, in the interest of the landholders, passed statutes enabling the justices of the peace to fix the rate of wages in each district, and providing for the punishment of the labourer who should ask, or the employer who should offer, more than this maximum. The laws of political economy could not be evaded, and selfish legislation only embittered but could not settle the dispute. This unwise "Statute of Labourers" (1352) was one of the main causes of the violent seditions among the agricultural classes which were to break out thirty years after.

CHAPTER IV.

FROM THE BLACK DEATH TO THE PEACE OF BRETIGNY, 1349-1360.

It was mainly owing to the frightful calamity of the Black Death, which fell with equal severity on France and England, that the war languished for the seven years which followed the appearance of the plague. For the greater part of the time there was a truce between the two countries. The suspension of arms negotiated in June, 1348, was periodically renewed, with an occasional short interval of hostilities. The armistice did not always prevent hostile encounters: while it was prevailing King Philip, late in the year 1349, made a desperate attempt to recover Calais by treachery. He offered Almerigo da Pavia, a mercenary captain who held a position of trust in the garrison, a great sum, 20,000 gold crowns, to admit

French troops within the castle by night. But the Italian met craft with craft, and revealed the scheme to King Edward, who hastily crossed from Dover with 900 men and took personal charge of the affair. Part of the French were allowed to enter, when the king and his men-at-arms fell upon them, and after a sharp fight captured or slew the whole body (Dec. 31, 1349).

A few months after this King Philip died (August 22, 1350), but the succession of his son John to the French crown made no change in international politics, for the new monarch would make no permanent peace with England, and continued his father's policy. Before he had been a week on the throne there was heavy fighting in the Narrow Seas. A great squadron of Biscayan ships passed up the Channel, committing many depredations on English commerce. King Philip had interested the King of Castile in his cause, and had induced him to send out his kinsman Charles, Count of La Cerda, at the head of this fleet, whose aims were half warlike, half commercial, for after passing the straits it put into the Flemish ports and loaded itself with merchandise. As it steered homewards King Edward put out from Sandwich with some ships which he had hastily collected, and fell upon it. The English were outnumbered, and their vessels were much smaller than those of the enemy. At first it seemed that they were likely to fare ill. Both the king's ship and that of his son, Edward Prince of Wales, were sunk by the enemies with whom they had grappled; but the crews clambered up from their sinking craft, and carried the Spaniards by boarding. After much desperate fighting, the strangers made off, leaving twenty-four of their vessels in the hands of the English. This fight, generally known by the name of *Espagnols-sur-Mer*, took place off Winchelsea on Aug. 29, 1350.

<small>Sea-fight with the Spaniards.</small>

The period before the renewed outbreak of open war with France was not unimportant in constitutional history. Besides the unwise *Statute of Labourers*, to which we have already alluded, and the *Statute of Provisors*, which resulted from the long quarrel with the pope which had opened in 1344, several other important pieces of legislation belong to the years 1350-1355. Among them were the *Statute of the Staple*, which provided that wool, leather, and fleeces, tin and lead, the most important English exports, should only be sold in certain towns, ten within the realm,[1] four in Ireland,[2] and two, Calais and Bruges, without it. The main object of this statute designating the staple-towns was to facilitate the levying of the duties on wool, which could be more easily collected if the king's officers had to keep their eyes on a small number of places only. But it harmed the small trading towns for the benefit of the greater ones, and put a dangerous monopoly in the hands of the "Merchants of the Staple", who were the only persons licensed to traffic in the designated places. Another important step was the passing of the *Statute of Treasons*, which defined more accurately than of old what offences fell under the head of treason—a necessary piece of work, for the judges of late had been trying to extend the meaning of the word, so as to get more profit from confiscations for the king. *Parliamentary legislation.*

The last of the series of truces which had followed the Black Death ran out on April 1st, 1355. In the summer of that year the English once more invaded France, hoping to have the aid not only of their old friends, the Montfort party in Brittany, but also of Charles the Bad, King of Navarre, whose broad estates in Normandy were conveniently placed for the receiving of English succours. But the great armament which Edward was to have taken to Normandy was beaten back by storms, and Charles of Navarre had to make peace with his cousin, King John, in order to avoid destruction. A second and smaller English army had been despatched to Bordeaux under the Prince of Wales, who had now reached his twenty-sixth year, and was intrusted with independent command. This force had better for- *Renewal of the French War.*

[1] London, Bristol, Canterbury, Chichester, Exeter, Lincoln, Newcastle, Norwich, York, Caermarthen.   [2] Dublin, Cork, Drogheda, Waterford.

tune than the king's host, and after landing and being joined by the forces of Gascony, executed a destructive raid into Languedoc. The Black Prince made his way past Toulouse, burning and harrying the countryside as far as Narbonne and Carcassonne, both of which places he plundered, till he almost reached the Mediterranean. This foray cut deeper into France than any English invasion before or after. But it had no result but plunder, and served no political or strategical purpose. Meanwhile the king had reorganized his storm-shattered host, and passed the seas to Calais in the late autumn. But as he was ravaging Picardy news was brought him that the Scots had taken Berwick by surprise and entered Northumberland. Much angered by the news, Edward abandoned his enterprise, and returned to his own realm to chastise the northern enemy. Though winter had come he crossed the border, and ravaged the Marches and Lothian, as far as Edinburgh, with great cruelty. So systematically did he set fire to all places great and small that the Scots remembered his invasion as "the Burnt Candlemas"—Candlemas day (Feb. 2) having fallen into the midst of his destructive march. No open opposition in the field was offered him, but his foraging parties were cut off, and his retreat to Berwick much harassed by the Lowlanders.

<small>Burnt Candlemas.</small>

In the summer of 1356 the Black Prince, who had earned the confidence of his followers by his successful raid into Languedoc, resolved to repeat his incursion of the previous year, and started from Bordeaux with an army of some 3500 men-at-arms and 4000 or 5000 infantry, of whom rather more than half were English, the rest of the force being composed of the feudal levies of Guyenne. This time he did not strike at southern, but at central France; he passed through the Limousin, Auvergne, and Berry, plundering far and wide till he came to the Loire. Apparently it was his purpose to co-operate with a smaller army under his younger brother, John of Gaunt, which had started from England on June 1st to land in Brittany. But this secondary expedi-

THE BLACK PRINCE'S RAID. 47

tion completely miscarried, though it was joined by some discontented Norman barons, the partisans of the King of Navarre.

Edward's own march met with no check till he had marched along the Loire almost as far as Tours. Then he heard that King John, with all the levies of northern and central France, was coming against him, and had crossed the river at Blois, with the intention of getting between the invaders and their base at Bordeaux. The prince's army was not a fifth of the strength of that of the French, and was clogged with a vast wagon train loaded with plunder. He did not, therefore, intend to fight, but made the best of his way homewards. The two hosts lost touch of each other for a space, but suddenly met again near Poictiers, where their lines of march crossed each other. Finding himself so close to the enemy that he could not get off without sacrificing all his booty, Edward halted and drew up his men on the hillside by the village of Maupertuis, with a hedge covering his front, the river Miausson to his left, and a thick wood behind him. He expected to be instantly attacked, but King John wasted a day in reconnoitring the English position and in sending in proposals that his enemies should surrender on terms. These were, of course, declined. Next day the prince thought he might succeed in slipping off to the rear without a fight, and had moved his baggage and his vanguard across the Miausson, when the French were seen advancing in four lines to assault the position. The English hastily got back into line of battle, and the fighting soon began.

The march to Poictiers.

King John, remembering the effect of the English arrows at Crecy on the French cavalry, had made the greater part of his men-at-arms dismount and march on foot in serried columns. Only his vanguard, chosen from the best knights in the army, were bidden to keep on their horses and ride in rapidly on the English archery, as a kind of forlorn hope; the rest came up on foot in three lines, each composed of 4000 or 6000 men, headed respectively by the Dauphin, the Duke of Orleans, and the

48   ENGLAND AND THE HUNDRED YEARS' WAR.

king himself. The devoted squadrons in front were led by Clermont and D'Audrehem, the two Marshals of France.

The Black Prince's force was now about 6000 strong; it was drawn up, as his father's host had been at Crecy, with two corps forming a front line and a third in reserve. The northern wing was headed by the Earls of Suffolk

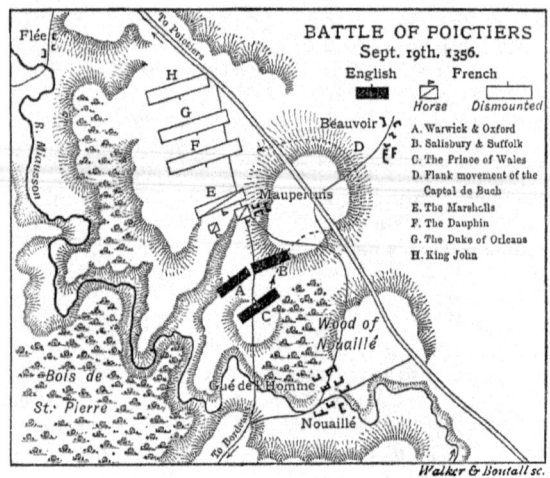

and Salisbury, the southern by the Earls of Warwick and Oxford. They had lined the hedge with their archers, while the men-at-arms stood behind to support them: in the reserve was the prince himself and the best of his Gascon vassals, Jean de Grailly, the Captal de Buch.

When the two marshals charged up to the hedge with their mounted men, almost the whole body were shot down by the bowmen before they could get to handstrokes. But the Dauphin's corps coming up just as the horsemen were disposed of, succeeded in closing with the English and waged a fierce struggle all along the line: the prince had to send forward some of his reserve before

they could be beaten off. The fugitives, falling back in utter rout, threw the line headed by the Duke of Orleans into disorder, and, instead of advancing, it left the field in company with the routed van. *Battle of Poictiers.*
But King John himself with his last line came forward with great steadiness, and his single corps was equal in numbers to the whole English army. The Black Prince saw that a desperate effort must be made, for the enemy were fresh, while his own men were almost tired out. Instead, therefore, of waiting to be attacked he put his last reserve into action, and bade the entire host charge downhill upon the French. One more precaution was taken: the Captal de Buch was ordered to take 300 men, to describe a long circuit to the northward, and to fall upon the flank and rear of the enemy when he should see the main battles fairly engaged.

This movement was destined to prove decisive. The French king kept his men together, and made head for a time against the wearied English, whose archers had now used up all their arrows, and were fighting hand to hand among the men-at-arms. But when the Captal's small corps suddenly charged in from the rear, crying "St. George! Guienne!" the French thought themselves surrounded, and broke and fled in panic fear. The king alone obstinately stood his ground, and was taken prisoner, along with his youngest son, Prince Philip. Poictiers was not such a bloody field as Crecy, though the Marshal Clermont, the Duke of Bourbon, and many other lords, perished. But it was specially noted for the number of noble captives who fell into the hands of the English: besides the king and his son, fourteen counts and 1900 knights had been obliged to yield themselves to mercy. The prisoners, indeed, were so numerous that their captors preferred to dismiss many of them on parole, when they had promised to ransom themselves, rather than to take the responsibility of keeping guard over them (19th Sep. 1356).

The capture of the king was destined to have the most important political consequences. When her sovereign lay captive in London, France was without a head, and civil troubles broke out on every side. The Dauphin, as regent, was unable to keep up the royal authority, and nearly perished himself in a seditious rising of the mob of Paris, who slew the Marshals of Normandy and Champagne before his very face. The mercenaries who had served King John, being no longer paid their hire, turned bandits and went plundering in great bands all over the countryside. Worst of all, the oppressed peasantry, driven wild by the misery of the times, burst out into an anarchic revolt against all constituted authority, and in many regions burnt every castle and manor and slew every man and woman of gentle blood on whom they could lay hands. It was only by a desperate struggle that the *noblesse* finally succeeded in putting them down. This bloody revolt is generally called the *Jacquerie*, from *Jacques Bonhomme*, the usual nickname of the French peasant. While the land was suffering from all these woes no opposition could be offered to the English, who ranged at their will through the land, and gained possession of many towns and castles. In short, the years 1356-7-8 were the most miserable that France had known since the old Viking invasions of the ninth century.

The Jacquerie.

Edward III. might perhaps have made further conquests if he had not consented to make a truce of two years with his prisoner, King John, for he wished to give him an opportunity of coming to terms, and making a definitive peace. John, who naturally detested the restraints of captivity, was eager to get free, and would have subscribed to almost any conditions. When a treaty was offered him ceding to England Normandy, Anjou, Maine, Poitou, and all the other lands which Henry II. had held in France two hundred years before, he was quite ready to grant the exorbitant demand, and set his seal to it. But his son the Dauphin Charles and the States-general very properly refused their assent (May, 1359). It was not worth while, even in the desperate state to which France was reduced, to buy back an indifferent king at the cost of so many fair provinces. The English had gained no secure foothold, save Calais, in northern France, and it was preposterous to require the cession of regions where they had proved altogether unable to establish themselves.

To put pressure on the regent Edward III. determined to launch a new invading army into France. His military reputation gathered around his standard many thousands of veteran mercenaries, and these, added to the strong English host which he brought over to Calais, composed an army double or treble the size of that which had fought at Crecy. It was estimated by the chronicles at 100,000 strong, but this figure is of course a gross exaggeration. In October, 1359, the king broke up from Calais, and marched through Picardy and Champagne, wasting the land, till he came to Rheims. He laid siege to the town, intending, it is said, to have himself anointed in its cathedral, where the kings of France had been wont to celebrate their coronation for many centuries. *Renewed invasion of France.* But Rheims held out, and Edward then made a sweep through northern Burgundy, and then turned westward towards Paris. He laid waste the suburbs of the capital, but did not sit down before it, the season and the weather being unfavourable. Next he announced his resolve to march into the fertile lands about the Loire, and there to rest his army, deferring the siege of Paris till the summer should have returned. Meanwhile the Dauphin had forbidden his followers to make any attempt to meet the English in the open, and had contented himself with holding the walled towns. But the country was suffering so frightfully that he and his counsellors resolved to make one more attempt to obtain terms from King Edward. His envoys met the invader at Bretigny, near Chartres, and there was signed the famous treaty which put an end to the first stage of the Hundred Years' War (May 8, 1360).

The terms which Edward now granted were more lenient than those which he had demanded in the preceding year, but they were still very heavy. He consented to give up his claim to the French throne, and to recognize John as its rightful occupant, but the compensation which he received was enormous. He was to obtain almost the whole of the ancient Duchy of Aquitaine, including the parts which had been lost by John and Henry III., and it was to be granted

Treaty of Bretigny.

to him as a free state, not as land owing feudal homage to the French crown. The English king was already in possession of Guyenne and Gascony: he now added to his portion Poitou, Aunis, Saintonge, Angoumois, the Limousin, Perigord, Quercy, and Rouergue, besides the feudal superiority over the counts of Foix and Armagnac. Nor was this all: in the north Ponthieu, the old heritage

of Eleanor of Castille, was restored to him, and the tract
round Calais was enlarged so as to include the whole of
the small county of Guisnes. Moreover, King John was
to pay for his personal ransom the enormous sum of
3,000,000 gold crowns, of which 600,000 were to be given
over at once, and the rest paid up by annual instalments
of 400,000 spread over six years. The Breton succession
was to be settled by equitable arbitration.

Probably the French were wise in accepting the treaty:
they needed peace at any price in order to save the realm
from the frightful anarchy in which it was plunged. On
the other hand, it is certain that Edward would have
done better to moderate his claims. He only obtained,
by the vast territorial cessions which he exacted, some
millions of disloyal and unwilling subjects, who were
certain to rebel at the first opportunity. He should have
been contented with the ancient English holding in
Guyenne, where the towns and most of the nobles were
well affected to the house of Plantagenet; his hold on
southern France was really weakened rather than strengthened by the new additions. Thus the treaty bore within
itself the seeds of future trouble; but for the moment it
appeared to put a splendid and successful conclusion to
the long war which had been raging since 1336.

For the moment the general aspect of affairs seemed
satisfactory, for the Scottish war had also been brought
to a close. Edward Balliol, who had no son, had ceded
his rights on the Scottish crown to the English monarch
in 1356, and in the following year Edward III. Treaty with Scotland.
acknowledged his prisoner David II. as right-
ful king of Scotland, and set him free on condition of his
paying a ransom of 100,000 marks,[1] which payment was
to be spread over ten years (Oct., 1357). The long-
disputed town of Berwick remained in the hands of the
English, but no attempt was made to insist on the cession
of the Eastern Lowlands, which had been made by Balliol
in 1333. Altogether this treaty was a far more statesmanlike achievement than that of Bretigny. On the one hand,

[1] £66,666, 6s. 8d.

Scotland obtained a much-needed repose after her long troubles, and was not again engaged in open war with England for nearly thirty years. Border affrays between the moss-troopers of the two countries could not be wholly prevented, but led to no serious conflict. Edward, on the other hand, was freed from the danger of Scottish attacks on his rear during his subsequent wars with France. But the friendly feeling which had prevailed between the two nations in the thirteenth century, before the invasions of Edward I., could not be renewed after sixty years of almost continuous war.

CHAPTER V.

FROM THE PEACE OF BRETIGNY TO THE RENEWAL OF THE FRENCH WAR. ENGLAND UNDER EDWARD III. THE SPANISH WAR. 1360-1369.

The Peace of Bretigny forms the high-water mark of King Edward's prosperity. He had still seventeen years to reign, but they were to be a period of growing troubles and gradual decline, corresponding to the decay of the king's own vigour and health. In 1360 Edward had reached the age of forty-eight, but he was already beginning to show signs of the wear and tear of his busy life: men grew old ere their time in those hard days. He was now the father of a very large family—he had eleven children, of whom five sons and three daughters survived. One of his main desires was to strengthen the crown by marrying his sons to the heiresses of the great baronial families, so as to concentrate as much of the feudal strength of England as he could in the hands of the royal family. His eldest son and heir, Edward, Prince of Wales, had

Family policy of Edward III. reached the age of thirty before he entered into wedlock; he chose as his wife a lady of his own age, his cousin, Joanna Countess of Kent, who inherited the estates of her father, Earl Edmund, the victim of Mortimer. She was a widow, having previously married Sir John Holland, by whom she had two sons, destined to be prominent figures in the next reign. The Black Prince's marriage seems to have been one of inclination—his wife had been known as "the fair maid of Kent", and all authorities unite to sing her praises. The matches into which his younger brothers entered seem to have been of their father's making rather than their own; several of them were wedded before they were well out of their boyhood. Lionel, the second surviving son of the king, was married to Elizabeth de Burgh, the greatest heiress in Ireland, who held in her own right the county of Ulster. After her early death he espoused as his second wife Yolande Visconti, daughter of the Lord of Milan. John of Gaunt, the next brother, made the most wealthy match of the whole family; when only nineteen he married Blanche of Lancaster, the heiress of Henry of Lancaster, the victor of Cadzand and Auberoche. She was in her own right Countess of Lancaster, Derby, Lincoln, and Leicester, and the estates which she brought to her husband were the broadest heritage in England. Edmund of Langley, the fourth surviving son of Edward III., married as his first wife a Spanish princess, as his second his eldest brother's stepdaughter, Joanna Holland. Lastly, Thomas of Woodstock, the youngest of the princes, obtained as his bride Eleanor Bohun, one of the two co-heiresses of the ancient earldom of Hereford. At different times Edward conferred on each of his sons the title of duke—a dignity hitherto unknown in England. The Prince of Wales was made Duke of Cornwall, Lionel Duke of Clarence, John Duke of Lancaster, Edmund Duke of York, and Thomas Duke of Gloucester.

Of the three daughters of Edward III. who reached adult years Mary married John V., the Montfort claimant to the duchy of Brittany, Margaret was wedded to John Hastings, Earl of Pembroke, and Isabella to Ingelram de Coucy, a French baron who served her father as a great captain of mercenaries: he was created Earl of Bedford.

During Edward's own lifetime the concentration of so many of the richest fiefs in the hands of his sons undoubtedly strengthened the crown and enfeebled the baronage to a corresponding extent. But he does not seem to have reflected that he was leaving an unenviable future to his successor, destined to have to deal with

Results of Edward's family policy. uncles and cousins who were not only very powerful territorial nobles, but also princes of the blood, with possible claims on the crown. In endowing his younger sons with such enormous power he was contributing his part towards making the Wars of the Roses possible. It was the excessive strength of the house of Lancaster which proved the ruin of Richard II., and in a later generation it was the over-greatness of the heir of the united lines of York, Clarence, and Mortimer which brought down the house of Lancaster to its bloody end. Edward does not seem in the least to have foreseen that though his own sons would obey and support him, the patriarch of their race, yet his grandsons would have no such feelings of loyalty to his eldest son's heir.

Meanwhile these dangers were still in the far future, and Edward seemed in 1360 the most successful sovereign of his age. His fame as a soldier was spread all over Europe, and the English, who before his time enjoyed no

Military renown of the English. special military repute, became the models of all Western Christendom. The soldiers trained in his wars, Sir John Chandos, Knolles, Manny, Thomas and William Felton, and the Gascon Jean de Grailly, the Captal de Buch, were reckoned the best knights of their day. Sir John Hawkwood, who had risen from the ranks to become a captain of adventurers, passed on into Italy with his band and carried the balance of power in the peninsula with him, as he served one state or another with the famous "White Company". This ascendency of the English in the field implied the predominance of infantry as the chief power in war, to the detriment of the feudal chivalry which had ruled Europe for the last five centuries. In the new system, whose first victories had been seen at Dupplin and

Halidon Hill, the knights descended from their steeds and formed a solid centre of resistance, while the yeomen with their deadly archery took the more active share in the repulse of the hostile attack. Edward III. must have the credit of applying this order of battle, which had originally been devised against the Scottish spearmen, to the discomfiture of the French feudal horse. The effect of Crecy and Poictiers was so great that the art of war in Western Europe was wholly revolutionized, and the French, Germans, and Italians took to dismounting and fighting on foot like the English. This loss of military ascendency by the *noblesse* was still further developed by another military change of the fourteenth century. Firearms, whose feeble beginnings go back to the first decade of Edward's reign, were slowly improving and coming into more general use all through the succeeding generation. Though their size was still small and their discharge slow, they proved almost as deadly to the feudal castle as the yeoman's arrow had been to the feudal horseman. It began to be possible to breach by the use of cannon strongholds which had hitherto been reckoned impregnable. This gave the king, the only person in the realm who possessed a competent train of artillery, an advantage in dealing with unruly barons such as he had never before enjoyed. Rebels could no longer rely on holding out behind their walls for many months, nor count starvation the only form of attack that they need dread. But the power of cannon to break up feudalism was only just beginning to be realized in the later days of Edward III.; it was not fully developed till the fifteenth century.

Edward III. did almost as much to advance the growth of English trade and commerce as to increase English military prestige. But his work in this province was not wholly intentional; when encouraging close commercial intercourse with Flanders he was thinking mainly of the political advantages of the connection with the Flemings, and also hoping to draw financial profits from the taxes on increased exports and imports. But there can be no doubt that his Netherlandish *Growth of commerce.*

and German alliances took Englishmen further afield than they had been wont to go before, and had favourable results on the national trade. Its volume increased so rapidly during the reign that Edward, first of all English kings,[1] was able to introduce a gold currency into the realm. Before his time the silver penny had been the largest monetary unit, but he succeeded in issuing with general approval a large gold coin called the Rose-noble, one of which exchanged for eighty pence. This broad, handsome piece secured such general acceptance that it circulated freely in the Netherlands and western Germany, and many of the lords and towns of the Low Countries took to striking money exactly imitating the noble in type and size.

This extension of the English currency is closely connected with the fact that from the time of Edward III. onward the English were beginning to send their own merchants abroad, and no longer were content to receive all continental goods at the home ports from foreign ships. Down to the fourteenth century the greater part of the sea-borne merchandise which England consumed was brought her by the Italians or the traders of the Hanseatic league. Edward very properly encouraged his subjects to sail abroad themselves, so as to get rid of the "middleman" and the charges which he exacted for transporting commodities to England. To compete with the powerful foreign trading societies the native merchants were bound together in the Company of "the Staple", whose institution we have already had occasion to notice. Though monopolies are generally harmful, yet in this case it was almost necessary to secure strength by combination, as the individual trader would have been helpless if he tried to oppose himself to the interests of the corporations of aliens whose markets he was invading. By the end of the century the limits of English seafaring trade were Lisbon and Ham-

The "Staple".

---

[1] Henry III. had tried to introduce a "gold penny", worth 20 silver pence, into circulation, but his subjects refused to take it—being apparently in no need of a coin of such high value, and the issue had to be withdrawn.

GROWTH OF ENGLISH TRADE. 59

burg; into the Mediterranean it did not yet penetrate, and the Baltic was almost entirely in the hands of the zealous Hanseatic league. But Chaucer's typical "shipman", as it will be remembered, knew all havens

"From Gothland to the Cape of Finisterre",

i.e. from north-western Spain to the coast of Sweden.

Manufactures were developing no less than trade. King Edward never did a wiser deed than when he invited the Flemish weavers to settle in Norwich, and make up on the spot the fine English wool which used formerly to be taken over to the Netherlands in order to be woven into cloth. In the true protectionist spirit a law of 1337 prohibited the wearing of any but English cloth by all persons save the royal family. Weaving was not the only craft which took a new start in the fourteenth century from the introduction of foreign teachers; metal work was much improved, and the use of glass in domestic architecture grew much more common.

The influence of the Black Death on trade and prices deserves notice. It not only raised the wages of the agricultural classes—in despite of the Statute of Labourers—but increased the selling value of all manufactured goods. While corn and other natural products of the soil remained at their old level of price, and while sheep and oxen rose only slightly in value, all things produced by skilled manual labour cost from 40 to 60 per cent more than they did before the great plague. This came, of course, from the fact that the artisans had been seriously reduced in numbers, so that the survivors were able to demand much higher prices for their handiwork. Since the cost of food remained the same as it had been before, the labouring classes were able to buy it of better quality and in greater quantity than of old, and their standard of comfort appreciably went up. The merchant profited as much, or more, from the enhanced selling value of his wares as he lost through having to pay higher wages to the artisans who manufactured them. On the other hand, the capitalist

Results of the Black Death.

land-owner was in a worse position than in the days before the Black Death, since his farm produce cost more in the item of labour, and yet sold for much the same money that it had in the first half of the century. Hence two tendencies had their rise: the landholder who had been wont to cultivate a large part of his estate himself as a home-farm under a bailiff—"in demesne" as the term then was—either abandoned the practice and let the demesne land at a rent to tenant farmers, or tried to turn his arable fields into pasture. For a greater profit was to be had from rearing sheep for their wool, the great staple product of England, than by growing any sort of corn. These changes, however, were only beginning to make themselves felt in King Edward's time; it takes many years to turn a simple race of conservative habits into new methods of life and husbandry.

The actual loss of population by the Black Death took many generations to repair; it seems to have been felt far more in some districts than in others. The southern and eastern counties suffered more in proportion than the western, and probably lost in consequence somewhat of the enormous superiority in wealth and importance which they had hitherto possessed. They still remained, however, the preponderant part of the realm.

Nine years were destined to elapse between the conclusion of the Treaty of Bretigny and the renewal of the war with France. They were on the whole a time of peace and prosperity for England; and, as is generally the case during such periods, there is little of importance to record in the domestic annals during their course. The intermittent quarrel with the papacy which had been going on for many years caused the renewal of the Statute of Provisors, and the confirmation of a Statute of *Præmunire*, so called because by it persons who took appeals to the pope at Avignon were warned beforehand (*præmuniti*) that they made themselves liable to be brought before the king's courts for showing contempt of his exclusive right of jurisdiction in England (1365). The writs addressed against such offen-

Statute of Præmunire.

STATUTE OF PRÆMUNIRE.

ders began with the words *præmunire facias*, and hence came the name of the statute. Some curious legislation against the wearing of clothing too good for their condition by the lower and middle classes bears witness to their growth in prosperity since the Black Death. Like all "sumptuary" laws it had no effect, and had soon to be abandoned. It is perhaps worth noting also that in 1362 English was made the official language of the law-courts, where Norman-French had hitherto prevailed.

The foreign affairs of the realm are of more importance, and from the first made it evident that the Treaty of Bretigny was to be a truce and not a permanent pacification. Its terms were never fully carried out. King John failed to raise his enormous ransom, and when he found that it could not be collected, loyally returned to England and surrendered his person, since he had failed to keep his promise. He died at the palace of the Savoy, in the Strand, on April 8th, 1364. When he had passed away his son Charles V., a very crafty and unscrupulous prince, refused to listen to any complaints as to the non-observance of the treaty. But he was as yet too busy in pacifying his own realm to stir against the English. He was not even firmly set upon the throne till the claims of his turbulent cousin, Charles the Bad of Navarre, were crushed by the defeat of Cocherel, and disposed of by a treaty signed in May, 1365.

Death of John of France.

The Breton war of succession, which had been raging ever since 1341, at last reached its termination in 1364. The younger John of Montfort, the ally of the English, at last succeeded in winning complete possession of his duchy by slaying his rival Charles of Blois at the battle of Auray, a fight gained by the valour and tactical skill of Sir John Chandos and the other English knights who served under his banner (September 29, 1364).

But another war in which England was interested was to lead to less happy results. It was the work of Edward the Black Prince, who had been ruling in Aquitaine almost as an independent prince since his father handed it over to him and gave him the ducal title in 1362. To

his court at Bordeaux there came as a suppliant an exiled Spanish prince, Pedro, King of Castile, whom his sub-
jects surnamed "the Cruel". He was a stern and high-handed prince, whose harsh and wicked rule—he had murdered his wife and one of his half-brothers among countless other victims—had driven the Castilians into revolt. The insurrection had been headed by his bastard brother, Henry, Count of Trastamara, who had called in to his aid a great host of French mercenaries led by Bertrand du Guesclin, a famous Breton captain of adventurers. Henry with the help of these allies easily expelled Pedro from his realm, and had himself crowned as king (1366). The exile urged on the Black Prince that his situation in Aquitaine would be perilous if he let the neighbouring Spanish lands pass under the control of a dependant of the French. He promised to repay all the expenses of the war if Edward would restore him to his throne, and to bind himself the closer to the English offered to leave his two daughters, Constance and Isabel, in the Black Prince's hands as hostages. After some hesitation Edward resolved to give the king his aid; the political advantages of the move influenced him much, but he was moved even more by a chivalrous impulse. He hated the idea of turning away a suppliant, and loving war for its own sake he was burning to add new laurels to those of Poictiers and Espagnols-sur-Mer.

Pedro the Cruel.

Accordingly he accepted Pedro's offer: and the nobles of Aquitaine were bidden to prepare for a Spanish war in the next spring. John of Gaunt brought over a small contingent from England, but the bulk of the army of invasion was made up of the Gascon *noblesse*, and the veteran mercenaries who flocked in from all quarters to join the prince's banner. So great was his warlike fame in Europe that more adventurers came to proffer him their aid than he could possibly feed or pay. He had to send away thousands of them, after having picked out the best of the men-at-arms to serve him. Thus his army was composed of

Prince Edward invades Castile.

none but choice troops, and far exceeded in military value the Spanish feudal levies against which it was to be pitted.

Edward crossed the Pyrenees by the pass of Roncesvalles—famous in history and in song for the defeat of the Emperor Charles the Great in 778, and for the death of Count Roland, the hero of the oldest legend of chivalry. Charles the Bad gave him a free passage through Navarre, and he did not see the enemy till he reached the hills above Vittoria, where Wellington was to win the crowning victory of the Peninsular War four and a half centuries later. Henry of Trastamara and his French allies had raised a great host which blocked the passes over the hills of Alava. But the prince outgeneralled them, slipped round their flank, and crossing the Ebro entered Old Castile. The Spaniards hurried back to place themselves between Edward's host and Burgos, the capital of the realm. The shock between the two armies took place in a broad level plain between the towns of Najera and Navarette. The result was never for a moment doubtful: though the Castilians were somewhat superior in numbers they were mostly raw troops; moreover they were accustomed to the skirmishing tactics of the Moors, not to facing the embattled line of dismounted men-at-arms flanked by archery. The great masses of light horsemen armed with buckler and javelin, which formed the most numerous part of Don Henry's host, broke and fled away in utter rout a few minutes after they came under the deadly shower of arrows. The French auxiliaries, who had sent away their horses and fought on foot (as at Poictiers), were surrounded, and slain or captured to the last man. The bastard, who had tried in vain to rally his scattered horsemen, fled away in haste and escaped into France (April 3, 1367). *Battle of Navarette.*

Thus Don Pedro recovered his kingdom at a single blow: he celebrated the victory by beheading such of the prisoners as fell into his hands, to the utter disgust of his chivalrous ally. Edward marched with him as far as

Burgos and replaced him in his palace, but dissensions at once began between them. Pedro could not or would not repay the vast sums which the prince had spent in raising and paying his army. The English host was kept cantoned round Burgos all through the summer, suffering severely from the unaccustomed heat, and from a lack of supplies. Sickness broke out among them, and Edward himself was prostrated by an attack of fever. Meanwhile the Castilian king had gone away to Andalusia, and sent evasive letters instead of remittances of money. At last the prince, in high disgust, marched back unpaid to Aquitaine, leaving his faithless ally to shift for himself. By displaying again his old cruelty and recklessness Pedro soon provoked a second rebellion of his subjects. Henry of Trastamara returned, defeated him in battle, and finally took him prisoner. The bastard then settled the succession question by brutally murdering his brother with his own hands (March, 1369).

Thus the only result of the victory of Navarette was that an implacable enemy of England was now firmly set Troubles in upon the Castilian throne, while the duchy Aquitaine. of Aquitaine was overwhelmed with the enormous debt incurred in restoring Don Pedro. The prince, honestly desiring to pay what he owed, sold his silver plate, surrendered to his followers the ransoms of his French and Castilian prisoners, and tried to make up the balance by raising money from his subjects. But his proposal to impose on every house in Aquitaine a hearth-tax of one franc provoked bitter opposition. The Poitevins and other newly-annexed vassals of the duchy were thoroughly discontented and disloyal, and took the first opportunity of withstanding their master. The estates of Aquitaine refused to vote the impost, and when Edward persevered in his plan, a body of barons, headed by the lords of Albret and Armagnac, announced their intention of appealing to the king at Paris. This was utterly contrary to the terms of the Treaty of Bretigny, by which Aquitaine had been freed for ever from all feudal dependence on the French crown. The Gascon nobles therefore had no right to call in Charles V.; but legality counted for little, and the one point of importance was to discover whether the king would dare to involve himself in a new English war, after the unhappy experiences of his father and grandfather.

Charles V. resolved to take the risk. He had got his realm into something like order during the five years which had elapsed since he had crushed the king of Navarre, and he was well acquainted with the fact that more than half of Edward's subjects in Aquitaine were ready to rebel and join him. Accordingly he first sent a summons to the Black Prince to appear at Paris and answer before his suzerain for wrongs done to the barons of the south, and when this preposterous order was ignored, commenced hostilities. It is said that, as a mark of contempt, he sent the final declaration of war not by a herald, as was the custom, but by the hands of his master-cook (April 29, 1369). *Renewed war with France.*

CHAPTER VI.

THE LAST YEARS OF EDWARD III. 1369–1377. THE LOSS OF AQUITAINE. DOMESTIC TROUBLES. RISE OF THE WYCLIFFITES.

From the very first moment of the outbreak of war, the struggle with France proved disastrous for England. Almost before the designs of Charles V. were realized news came that the isolated county of Ponthieu had been overrun by the enemy, and that Abbeville and its other towns and castles had surrendered. The state of affairs in Aquitaine was not much better: in many parts of Poitou, Perigord, and Rouergue powerful barons disavowed their allegiance, and took up arms in behalf of the French king.

In the war which followed the English lacked the advantage which they had enjoyed in the earlier struggle, of being guided by a single leader: King Edward never again took the field: though only in his fifty-eighth year, he was worn out as much in mind as in body.

The king's decline.

The direction of affairs ought to have passed to his eldest son, a man in the prime of life verging on his fortieth year. But the Black Prince had never recovered from the effects of the fever which had stricken him down during his Spanish campaign. For the rest of his life he was a confirmed invalid, and every exertion which he made was immediately followed by a relapse, which sent him back to his sick-bed. For the first two years of the war he endeavoured to stay at the helm, but the want of vigour and combination which attended the movements of the English troops showed that he was not himself. When he finally was obliged to retire from the scene of action in 1370, the main part of the responsibility fell to his next surviving brother, John of Gaunt, a busy and ambitious but not a capable prince. He had made many enemies, and was never able to command the same unhesitating obedience which had been shown to Edward III. and the Black Prince.

As long as the younger Edward still kept his court at Bordeaux the English continued to defend Aquitaine, with moderate success. But Sir John Chandos, the prince's right-hand man, was killed in a petty skirmish in Poitou, on December 31st, 1369, and after his death things took a turn for the worse. In 1370 the French struck deep into the duchy of Aquitaine, and captured first the strong town of Aiguillon in Agenois, and then the important city of Limoges, whose citizens treacherously opened their gates to the invaders. The prince took the field for the last time to recover Limoges, though he was so weak that he could not sit his war-horse, and had to be borne on a litter. He took the place after an obstinate defence, by throwing down part of the wall by a mine filled with gunpowder. When his men entered the breach he bade them cut down everyone they met, for he was much enraged with his rebellious subjects. Thus his hitherto spotless career

Capture of Limoges.

was sullied by a massacre in its last moments (October, 1370). Three months later his health grew so much worse that he took ship for England, expecting every moment to be his last. But he survived the passage, and lingered on for more than five years at his castle of Berkhampstead, a helpless invalid, unable to take any part either in war or domestic governance.

With the departure of the prince things in France went from bad to worse. The French could not be kept back from overrunning Aquitaine, though two considerable expeditions had been sent out from Calais to endeavour to distract them from their prey. But by the orders of their king the nobles of northern France utterly refused battle, shut themselves up in their castles, and allowed the English to march past them unmolested. These unchivalrous but effective tactics caused John of Gaunt, in 1369, and Sir Robert Knolles, in 1370, to march across Picardy without effecting anything of note, for they had no leisure to engage in sieges, and they could not get the battle that they desired.

But in 1372 England made a serious effort to reinforce Aquitaine. The Parliament had granted the king a subsidy of £50,000, and with it a considerable army and fleet was collected, and placed under the orders of John Earl of Pembroke, the king's son-in-law. He crossed the Bay of Biscay safely, but as he drew near La Rochelle, the port for which he was aiming, found his path beset by a large Spanish fleet. Henry of Trastamara was bent on revenging Navarette, and he had just Defeat off found another reason for taking strong mea- La Rochelle. sures against the English. John of Gaunt and his younger brother Edmund of Langley had in the winter of 1371-72 wedded the two daughters and heiresses of Pedro the Cruel, who had been dwelling as hostages at Bordeaux ever since their father broke his word in 1367. In virtue of this marriage John gave himself out as the rightful king of Castile. Henry was much enraged, and had sent forth to aid the French all the ships that he could gather together. A fierce fight ensued off La

Rochelle, in which the English were totally defeated, many of their light vessels being sunk by the great stones and masses of iron which the Biscayans cast down into them from their taller ships (June 22, 1372). Pembroke and many scores of knights were taken prisoners.

The defence of Aquitaine, now that the army of succour had been destroyed, fell upon the shoulders of the Captal de Buch, the loyal Gascon baron who had so much distinguished himself at Poictiers sixteen years before. He made a gallant fight, but was utterly unable to stem the advancing flood of French invasion. His forces were too small, and the discontented people of the land would give him no help. Poictiers, Niort, and La Rochelle fell into the hands of the enemy, betrayed by their citizens, and with them went almost the whole of Poitou, Saintonge, and the Angoumois. At last the Captal was surprised and taken prisoner in a skirmish near Soubise, and with him departed the last hope of maintaining the English dominion north of the Garonne. About the same time John V. of Brittany, the one faithful ally of King Edward, saw the greater part of his duchy overrun by the French, whose forces were led by his own born subject, the great *Condottiere* Bertrand du Guesclin, who had now been made Constable of France (1372-73).

In 1373 England made her last effort to turn the fortune of war. John of Gaunt was sent over the water with 3000 men-at-arms and 6000 bowmen; at Calais he was joined by a great body of mercenaries raised in the Netherlands and Germany. We hear to our surprise that he had even enlisted 300 Scottish lances to serve against the French. Thus a formidable army was mustered, but it was led by an incompetent general, and was directed on the wrong lines. It would have been better to start from Bordeaux, and clear Perigord and Saintonge of the enemy, instead of starting on a mere destructive raid into northern France. The experience of 1369 and 1370 had already shown that such operations had no effect against a king like Charles V., who did not intend to fight, and could not

John of Gaunt's great march.

JOHN OF GAUNT INVADES FRANCE. 69

be stirred to indiscretion even by seeing the barns and cottages of his subjects blazing up on every side. John of Gaunt was allowed to push his way across Picardy and Champagne as far as the Loire: the French hung about his route and cut off his stragglers, but would not offer battle. Then he moved on into Berri, and went on ravaging the land on his way to Bordeaux. The autumn had now set in, and among the rugged mountains of Auvergne the army suffered terrible privations: nearly all the horses died of starvation, and many men fell by the way from cold and over-fatigue. At last they reached Bordeaux ragged and famished, after having accomplished no useful end whatever: they had inflicted untold misery on the peasantry of central France, but had brought no pressure to bear on Charles V., nor even retaken one of the lost towns of northern Aquitaine. In April, 1374, Lancaster disbanded the remnants of his host, since he could no longer pay them, and returned to England.

The failure of his ill-managed expedition was followed by the loss of the greater part of Guyenne and Gascony. The inhabitants felt that the king of England's last bolt was shot, and that there was no object in fighting any longer for a lost cause. One after another all the towns along the Garonne and Dordogne gave themselves up to the French after feeble and perfunctory resistances. By the end of 1374 all that was left to King Edward was the cities of Bordeaux and Bayonne, and the narrow slip of Gascon coast-land connecting them: all the inland was gone. That the two great seaports still held out was mainly due to the fact that their trading interests were closely bound up with the English connection, and that they knew that they were getting better and more orderly government from their actual lord than would be granted them by Charles V. It must be remembered too that they had been in the hands of the Plantagenets ever since Henry II. had married Eleanor of Aquitaine two hundred years before, and had no historical nor sentimental ties with the house of Valois.

The English in Guyenne.

Considering the utter ruin of the English cause in

Aquitaine, Edward III. must be considered to have been fortunate when in the June of the following year (1375) he succeeded in concluding a suspension of hostilities with the enemy. The truce was for a year, but it was renewed for a second twelvemonth in June 1376, and actually lasted for the whole of the short remainder of the old king's reign.

The five years during which Aquitaine was gradually passing into the hands of the French were very important in the constitutional history of England. All through their course a bitter struggle was going on in Parliament, caused by the discontent of the nation at the unfortunate issue of the war. Its first sign was an outbreak against the king's ministers in 1371. It was easy to attribute the successes of the French to the incapacity of the men whom the king had chosen to carry on the administration: of these the most important were two prelates, William of Wykeham bishop of Winchester, the chancellor; and Thomas of Brantingham bishop of Exeter, the treasurer. Both were able and disinterested men: Wykeham, who had first attracted Edward's attention by his skill as an architect, had been found an honest and capable statesman, and has left a good name behind him as the founder of Winchester College, the first great public school, and of the sister foundation of New College, Oxford. It was wholly unjust to lay the blame of the losses in Aquitaine on the chancellor and treasurer; they were really due to military causes—the want of a single competent general-in-chief, and the squandering of men and money on the unwise raids into northern France. But the Parliament attributed them to the incapacity of ecclesiastics to rule in time of war, and petitioned the king to dismiss them, and to replace them by laymen. Edward yielded, and Sir Robert Thorpe was made chancellor, while Sir Richard Scrope, a follower of John of Gaunt, took over the charge of the treasury.

Troubles in Parliament.

The new administration proved far more unfortunate than that which it had supplanted. John of Gaunt had now become the true ruling power in the realm: his elder brother was on his sick-bed, and his father was falling into his dotage. Edward III. had lost his wise and faithful wife, Philippa of Hainault, in 1369, and shortly after fell into the hands of a worthless adventuress, Dame Alice Perrers. In his foolish fondness for her he allowed her to tamper with matters of state, and all who wished to advance themselves about the court came to her with bribes. She even contrived to interfere with the administration of justice, and to frighten or corrupt the judges. John of Gaunt left his father in the hands of this harpy, and assumed complete control of foreign affairs. It was on him that the responsibility for the disasters of 1373-4-5 must be laid. After the loss of Guyenne he was forced to face Parliament with a lamentable report of money wasted, opportunities let slip, and provinces lost to the French.

Corruption of the court.

On the meeting of the "Good Parliament" of 1376 the storm of national discontent, which had been brewing for the last three years, burst upon Lancaster's head. He was accused justly enough of incapacity, but men added unfounded accusations, such as the charge of plotting to seize the throne at his father's death, to the exclusion of his invalid brother, and of the little prince Richard, the Black Prince's nine-year-old son. It was even whispered that he had planned to get the boy poisoned. John himself was too highly placed for the Parliament to dare to attack him openly, but a vigorous assault was made on his friends and associates. Peter de la Mare, the speaker of the House of Commons, boldly declared that the nation was ready to help the king in his distress, but that they must first remove from about his person those who were making their private profit out of his misfortunes. The three chief offenders pointed out were the chamberlain, William Lord Latimer, Richard Lyons, the king's financial agent, and Dame Alice Perrers. The two first-named had been guilty of disgraceful frauds; they had bought up the king's debts, from poor men who despaired of ever seeing their money, at half their nominal amount or less, and had then paid

The Good Parliament.

themselves in full from the treasury. On one occasion they had lent the king 20,000 marks (£13,333, 6s. 8d.), and got out of him an acknowledgment for £20,000 sterling. Latimer had extorted a great bribe from the Duke of Brittany, England's faithful ally, and had then betrayed him by selling his castles of St. Sauveur and Becherel to the French. Latimer and Lyons were accordingly *impeached*, *i.e.* formally accused by the Commons and tried by the House of Peers. The Lords found them guilty, and they were sentenced to be fined, imprisoned, and deprived of their offices. Several minor offenders were punished at the same time. As to Dame Alice, the Commons accused her of breaking the law which forbade women to meddle with the administration of justice, and obtained against her an award of banishment. She was made to swear that she would never return to the king's presence, an oath which she very soon broke.

While these trials were in progress the Prince of Wales died (June 8, 1376). Parliament petitioned the king that his little grandson Richard should be at once recognized as heir to the crown, and that a standing council should be appointed to carry on the government. Edward himself was no longer capable of work, and it was felt that John of Gaunt must be prevented from engrossing all the royal powers into his hands. Accordingly the king consented that Parliament should nominate nine persons as members of the council, of whom at least four were to be always about his person. At the same time, he promised to consider favourably the demands contained in a vast list of 140 petitions, dealing with all manner of administrative grievances, which the Commons laid before him. Two of the most important of these documents demanded, the one that Parliaments should be annual, the other that the sheriffs and other royal officers should not interfere with the election of knights of the shire, but always allow the return of the persons whom "the better folk of the county" should nominate.

On the 6th of July the Parliament dispersed, having, as it fondly supposed, crushed Lancaster and provided for the future good governance of the realm. The moment that they had broken up, John of Gaunt took his revenge, and executed a kind of *coup d'état*. He got his doting father into his hands, and then used his name to declare that the "Good Parliament" had been no parliament at all, and that its acts were null and void. He threw the late speaker, Peter de la Mare, into prison, dismissed the nine newly-appointed councillors, and released Lyons and the other culprits who had been condemned. Alice Perrers was allowed quietly to return to court.

John of Gaunt recovers power.

A new Parliament was then summoned to meet, and, by employing the royal prerogative in the most unscrupulous fashion, and threatening and overawing the electors, Lancaster succeeded in getting returned a large majority of his supporters (January, 1377). The king had now entered into the fiftieth year of his reign, and to celebrate his jubilee proclaimed a pardon and amnesty to many minor offenders and debtors. At the head of the list, however, appeared the names of Latimer and Lyons and their underlings, who were relieved of all fines, penalties, and disabilities which had been laid upon them in the previous year.

All these actions were scandalous and highly calculated to lead to civil war. If the party which opposed the duke and the court had been headed by a baronial chief of the type of Simon de Montfort, or of the great earls who had withstood Edward I., it is probable that Lancaster would have been overthrown by force of arms. But this was far from being the case: the most prominent leader of the constitutional party was Bishop William of Wykeham, a lover of peace and caution; and the chief lay patron of the cause, the young Earl of March, was also a man of moderate views. No open opposition to Duke John was made at first, even when he proceeded to bring against Wykeham a ridiculous charge of embezzling public funds, as a kind of counterblast to the impeachment of Latimer and Lyons in the preceding year.

Lancaster, though a short-sighted politician, was yet

conscious that he must soon be overthrown unless he could manage to enlist a certain amount of popular sympathy on his side. The truce with France being still running he could not appeal to warlike sentiments, but there was one strong current of opinion which he thought that he might direct into channels favourable to himself.

This was the anti-papal feeling, which was as strong now as in the days when the Statutes of Provisors and Præmunire had been passed. The court of Avignon was going from bad to worse, and its shameless demands and exactions deeply irritated every patriotic Englishman. But a great part of the clergy, now as always, thought themselves bound to side with the papacy, and the English Church was itself full of abuses and scandals, which did not tend to grow less. Bishops who neglected their dioceses, and were more at home in war and diplomacy than in spiritual work, had always existed, but in the fourteenth century their numbers were greater than ever, since the baronage had taken of late to putting their younger sons into the church and pressing them forward for promotion. In earlier centuries this had been rare, in the fourteenth it was very common. Three of the seven Archbishops of Canterbury between 1348 and 1400 were sons or brothers of peers. The average of episcopal piety and unworldliness was not improved by the change. Among the beneficed clergy there was a good deal of non-residence, an appreciable amount of simony, and a certain proportion of evil-living. The abbeys and friaries were worse: all accounts agree that the monastic bodies were inferior to the secular priests in zeal and moral worth. It is said that the hasty filling-up of the depleted ranks of the clergy with unqualified and unsatisfactory persons after the Black Death had a permanent effect in lowering the moral tone of the whole body. At the same time the church was richer than ever: it was believed that a third of the land and wealth of the realm were in clerical hands. The clergy always gave liberal grants in convocation for national purposes, but this did not satisfy men who complained that their land escaped all feudal taxation, and so did not pay its fair share towards filling the treasury.

The feeling that something ought to be done to improve the internal condition of the church, as well as to check the encroachments of the pope, had long been prevalent, and was shared by many who were themselves clerics. Among those who were foremost in calling for radical measures of reform was John Wycliffe (sometime Master of Balliol College), a learned Oxford doctor of divinity. He had first made his mark as a deep thinker in philosophy and theology, but was driven into politics by his indignation at the corrupt state of the church and the papacy. He came to the conclusion that most of the clerical scandals of the day had their roots in the over-great wealth and power of the church, and held that the best way to reform it would be to compel the clergy to return to the apostolic poverty of the early centuries. Against the papacy, as the source of all other evils, he was particularly keen. He had been first introduced to public affairs as a member of a deputation sent to Bruges in 1374 to negotiate terms of agreement between the English Church and the pope. The evil impression which the papal delegates then made on him he never forgot. Ere long we find him protesting in the strongest terms against the spiritual authority which the pope claimed to exercise over the whole church, and asserting that it was blasphemous for him to pose as God's vicegerent on earth, and the mediator between Christ and the individual Christian. "All men", he said, employing a familiar metaphor drawn from the feudal system, "are tenants-in-chief under God, responsible directly to him for their souls and their manner of life; the pope is like an intruder who tries to push in as a mesne-tenant between God and man." Then he added that spiritual authority could only be wielded by a righteous man, and that no obedience was due to the orders of a spiritual ruler whose life was not in consonance with the word of Christ. Not

Wycliffe.

Wycliffe's teaching.

only the pope, but a large number of the English prelates might fairly be said to come under this condemnation. At a later date Wycliffe added to his attack on the governors of the church an attack on some of the characteristic doctrines of Rome, notably on that of Transubstantiation in the Eucharist.

This later development, however, had not begun in 1377, and it was only as preaching insubordination and resistance to Rome that Wycliffe was at this time arraigned and tried by Bishop Courtenay of London, a strong opponent of John of Gaunt. The duke's only sympathy with Wycliffe came from the fact that they both desired to repress the overgrown power of the ecclesiastical authorities, the one from political and personal motives, the other on religious and theoretical grounds. With Wycliffe's spiritual fervour Lancaster had nothing in common, but he resolved to support him because they owned the same enemies, and because there was always popularity to be gained by opposing Rome.

Accordingly when Wycliffe was brought before the bishop in St. Paul's for trial (February, 1377) the duke came in person, and threatened Courtenay in such stormy language that after an unseemly altercation the assembly broke up in disorder, and Wycliffe went free. A mob of the bishop's friends and followers went next day and sacked John's palace of the Savoy. Though much enraged he dared not proceed to more violent measures against Courtenay, and contented himself with making his father suspend for a time some of the privileges of the city of London.

Trial of Wycliffe.

Thus the political strife of the Court party and the Constitutional party had become complicated with the religious dispute between the Reformers and the Romanizers. How much further matters would have gone had John of Gaunt retained his unlimited power and authority we cannot say, for the aspect of affairs was wholly changed a few months later by the death of the old king. Edward died on June 2, 1377, at his palace of Sheen. When his last moments were near his servants stole all they could and fled. The shameless Alice Perrers is said to have stripped the very rings from his hands when she saw him fall into unconsciousness. Of all the numerous train that he had fed only one poor priest was present to minister the offices of the church as he drew his last breath. This miserable death-bed was but the natural termination of a life spent in the pursuit of selfish pleasure and ambition. Such a king was bound to breed a race of heartless courtiers and thankless dependants.

Death of Edward III.

CHAPTER VII.

RICHARD II. THE YEARS OF THE MINORITY. 1377–1388.

The accession to the throne of the late king's grandson, Richard II., a bright promising lad of eleven, put an end to the domination of John of Gaunt. The Princess of Wales and the friends of her deceased husband, who had brought up the young king, had never been allied to Lancaster, and had viewed his movements with suspicion. He had no longer the power to use the royal name for his own profit as he had done for the last few years. Facing the situation with more wisdom than might have been expected, the duke made no attempt to hold on to the helm, but yielded with a good grace, and entered into a formal reconciliation with Wykeham and the other chiefs of the constitutional party. Peter de la Mare was released from prison, the Londoners were pardoned for their riot of the preceding February, and it was agreed that old enmities should be forgotten. The governance of the realm was placed in the hands of a council in which both the parties were fairly represented. The first parliament of the new reign passed two important pieces of constitutional legislation: one provided that during a minority the king's ministers should be chosen by the two houses; the other was to the effect that all acts passed by Parliament could be set aside only by the consent of Parliament. This second point was one which was not to be fully established for three hundred years. As late as the time of James II. kings still claimed to have a dispensing power which overrode the statute-book.

Though the danger of domestic troubles was for a time at an end, the condition of politics was yet far from satisfactory. Charles V. of France had refused to renew the truce which ran out in the summer of 1377, and the "Hundred Years' War" had once more passed into an acute stage. The campaigns which followed were neither so disastrous nor so decisive as those of 1373-75, but their results were on the whole unfavourable. Nothing of importance was lost — the whole inland had already fallen into the hands of the French, and the grasp of the English on the coast towns was very firm—but, on the other hand, nothing was regained, and the expenses of the war were ruinous. In 1380 an expedition under the king's youngest uncle, Thomas of Woodstock, landed at Calais, and cut its way through Picardy, Champagne, and the Orleanois to Brittany. It was a mere repetition of Lancaster's march in 1373: once more the French avoided open battle, and contented themselves with defending their walled towns and cutting off the foragers and stragglers of the invading host. Earl Thomas reached Vannes without any overwhelming disaster, but with an army too much harassed and worn down to accomplish the delivery of Brittany from the French. John V., the faithful ally of England since his accession in 1345, was at last driven to abandon the alliance and make peace with the enemy. He was recognized as duke by the French government in return for his submission, and at last recovered the whole of his dominions (1380).

The French war.

The abortive expedition to Brittany had been very costly, and heavy taxation was necessary to pay the troops, whose wages were six months in arrear. Accordingly the chancellor, Simon of Sudbury, Archbishop of Canterbury, laid before the Parliament of Northampton projects for the raising of a

The Poll-tax of 1381.

sum of £160,000. The method finally adopted for collecting it was a Poll-tax on the whole of the inhabitants of the realm above the age of fifteen: it was graduated upwards from one shilling paid by the poor, to £3 imposed on the richest individuals.

The imposition of this tax, which pressed very heavily on the labouring classes, was the cause of the explosion of a discontent which had been brewing ever since the social troubles that had followed the Black Death and the Statute of Labourers. The Peasant Revolt, or Wat Tyler's Rebellion, as it is sometimes called, was not the result of the Poll-tax only. That imposition, though bitterly resented, was but the occasion and not the cause of the rising—just as the greased cartridges in 1857 were not the cause of the Indian Mutiny. The origins of the trouble were many, and varied much in different places. In London and the towns the discontent was largely political; the people resented the disastrous results of the French war, and the heavy taxation which resulted from it. They laid the blame on the governing classes, without much distinction of persons and parties, save that John of Gaunt was specially singled out as responsible for the present unhappy situation. In the shires, on the other hand, the explosion was mainly the result of social causes, and especially of the grievances of villeinage. We have had already *Causes of the Peasant Revolt.* occasion to remark that the Statute of Labourers had estranged the landholders from their peasants. The attempt to enforce the ancient dues of compulsory labour from the servile tenants had led to much bad blood: everyone wished to hold his land at a moderate money rent, and not to be compelled to give forced labour for his lord's demesne farms. Wherever the owner of a manor insisted on carrying on the old system discontent was rife. In many parts the peasantry had entered into secret clubs and combinations to resist their masters, and these societies seem to have had much to do with the organization of the rising. But this grievance alone does not suffice to explain the revolt: its outbreak was as violent in Kent, where villeinage no longer existed, as in any other shire. There was a bitter feeling abroad against the tyrannical forest laws, against the tolls and market dues which raised the price of provisions, against the whole tribe of lawyers, whose subtilties and legal fictions were thought to prevent the poor man from obtaining justice. In some parts, too, the rising was strongly anti-clerical: it was very violent in places like St. Albans and Bury St. Edmunds, where the tenants of the church had tried in vain to get from their abbots the charters and privileges which most other small towns enjoyed. Very important also (though it has sometimes been exaggerated) was the influence of Wycliffe's denunciation of the clergy during the last ten years. His teaching had filtered down to the lower strata of society in a form which took the shape of socialism. He had preached that obedience was not due to spiritual superiors of evil life, and that it was expedient that the church should be deprived of the over-great wealth which was corrupting her. He had founded an order of "poor priests" who went about the country spreading his doctrines, and in the mouths of his more fanatical disciples his teaching took an almost anarchical turn. They denounced all obedience to un-righteous governors, lay or clerical, and spoke as if poverty was the only virtue and riches the sole source of evil. The most violent language of this kind was used by a wandering priest named John Ball, who was well known all over the southern shires. He was not a Wycliffite, since he had been in trouble for his teaching long before Wycliffe's name had been heard outside Oxford, but his addresses pressed to their logical extreme all the ideas which underlay the new doctrine. His famous text:

> "When Adam delved and Eve span,
> Who was then the gentleman?"

was the prelude to sermons urging that all men must be made equal, and all property forcibly divided into equal shares. For the most part, however, the men who joined in the revolt were not bent on setting the whole world to rights, but on getting rid each of his own special grievance.

In June, 1381, the rising broke out in all the eastern counties, from Kent as far as Yorkshire, with a simultaneity that shows that it must have been prepared beforehand. Whether the organization had been made by the secret societies of the labourers or by the travelling agitators is not certain, though we know that John Ball had held a meeting in London, just before the rising, with some of the men who afterwards led the revolt in Norfolk and Suffolk. The first riot broke out, it is said, at Dartford, in Kent, where a certain tiler slew one of the collectors of the poll-tax who had grossly insulted his daughter. Whatever may be the truth of this story, it is certain that all Kent rose in arms as if on a given signal, and a few days afterwards Essex and the eastern counties followed suit (June, 1381). *The first rising.*

In all the regions over which the rising spread there was a certain amount of bloodshed and a good deal of plunder. The persons who were slain were mainly justices of the peace, lawyers, and officials connected with the levying of the poll-tax. But local quarrels and grievances led to other murders, such as those of the Prior of Bury St. Edmunds and the Governor of Norwich Castle. Everywhere the manors of unpopular landlords were sacked, and manor rolls and records of taxation sought out and burnt. In Cambridge, where the town and the university had an old quarrel, the mob burst open the university church and burnt all the charters and muniments, crying, "Away with the learning of clerks! away with it!"

After a few days of uproar the bands of the home counties began to move on London. Those of Kent, under a leader who called himself Wat Tyler, encamped on Blackheath, while the men of Hertfordshire took post at Highbury, and those of Essex at Hampstead. They all agreed in swearing that they were true to the king, and only desired to deliver him from his evil counsellors.

The gates of London were shut against them by the Mayor Walworth, but there was no other attempt to resist them, for the government had been taken by surprise, and had no time to collect troops. But on June 12 the mob of the city rose and opened the gates to the insurgents. They spread themselves through the streets, not indulging in general plunder, but sacking and burning the Savoy, the palace of John of Gaunt, and slaying many foreign merchants and certain persons against whom they had special grievances. The young king, who had retired into the Tower, tried to parley with them. The demands which they sent him were not so wild as might have been expected: they asked for a free pardon, for the abolition of all villeinage, for the removal of many taxes and tolls, and for a permission to all who had formerly held land on a servile tenure to become instead free tenants of their farms at the rent of fourpence an acre. It is evident that the majority had not been led away by the teaching of John Ball and his fellows. Seeing that their terms were not altogether impossible, the young king,—who displayed admirable courage and coolness, though he was but fifteen years of age,—bade them meet him at Mile End, then a great open space, and there discuss their grievances. The majority came to the colloquy; but while it was going on Wat Tyler and John Ball, with about 400 riotous followers, burst into the Tower, and there murdered the Archbishop Simon of Sudbury, who was specially hated as the framer of the poll-tax, and with him Sir Robert Hales, the treasurer, and John Legge, the chief collector of the tax.

The rebels in London.

Murder of Archbishop Sudbury.

While this dreadful scene was going on, the young king had been addressing the main body of the insurgents at Mile End. After some discussion, he agreed to grant their demands, and thirty clerks were set at once to work to draw out charters granting free pardons and the abolition of villeinage for the inhabitants of each town or hundred. That evening the majority of the insurgents went quietly home, having, as they thought, obtained their desires (June 13). But Tyler and many thousands of the rougher and wilder sort remained behind: some of them were fanatics, and others were scenting more plunder and bloodshed.

Next day the king summoned Tyler and his followers to meet him at Smithfield, trusting to make terms with them as he had with their fellows. But the insurgent chief had gone too far to feel himself safe, and was set on keeping up the tumult, lest he should be called to justice for the murders of Sudbury and Hales. He bore himself insolently at the meeting, and began wrangling and insulting the king's attendants. This so excited William Walworth, the mayor, that he drew a cutlass from under his gown and hewed down the rebel from his horse. Thereupon one of the king's squires ran in and struck him dead as he lay. *King Richard at Smithfield.* Richard and his whole party were within an ace of perishing, for the multitude, seeing their leader fall, bent their bows, and were about to let fly. But the courageous young king rode forward among them, crying that he himself would now be their leader, and would see that justice was done to them. They hesitated a moment, and then, won by his noble bearing, followed him to Islington, where, in the open field, he distributed to them charters like those which had been given to their fellows on the previous day. They then dispersed, and he was able to ride back to his mother swearing "that he had this day won back his heritage and the realm of England, which was lost" (June 14).

When the insurgents had gone home the knights and nobles flocked into London, with thousands of armed retainers. The land-holding classes were very wroth that their villeins had been freed without their consent, and said that Richard had given away what was not his own. In spite of the free pardon that had been granted, many scores of the leaders of the *Reaction and revenge.* rebels in Kent and the home counties were seized and hung. Among them were John Ball, and "Jack Straw", who had been captain of the Essex men. In Norfolk the warlike bishop Despenser took arms and put down the eastern insurgents, slaying their leader, the priest John Wrawe. A few months later Parliament met, and voted that all the charters issued by the king were null and void, because they had been issued without the sanction of the two houses. Richard made some attempt to keep his promise to the insurgents, and tried to get his abolition of villeinage confirmed, but the voice of Lords and Commons was given unanimously against him, and he had to yield. The only grace that he obtained was that in January, 1382, on the occasion of his marriage to Anne of Bohemia, the young daughter of the Emperor Charles IV., a general amnesty was published for the surviving insurgents. But all their prominent leaders had already perished. Nevertheless, it must not be forgotten that in one way the rising had not been without successful results; the land-owning classes had been so thoroughly frightened by the outbreak that they dealt more cautiously with the peasants for the future; for the next century villeinage was silently disappearing, as the lords allowed their men to commute labour for money rents, and to become free tenants. The grievances of villeinage were never again the cause of insurrection, for they gradually disappeared. In the next century, we shall see that the great popular rising of Jack Cade, which in many features recalls that of Wat Tyler, was political and not social in its aims and ends.

Richard was now in his sixteenth year, and had shown that he possessed both courage, ready wit, and a heart that could sympathize with his subjects. But he was not allowed to assume control of the administration; all through his reign he was the victim of a tribe of ambitious uncles and cousins, who were determined to keep him in the background as much as possible. John of Gaunt was now not the only source of trouble; his youngest brother, Thomas of Woodstock, who had become Duke of Gloucester, was a far worse man — domineering, arrogant, selfish, and given to all manner of intrigues. He and Lancaster fell out, and

Thomas of Gloucester.

their quarrels allowed the king some liberty; but in 1385 the elder duke disappeared for some time from the scene. By his marriage with Constance of Castile[1] he had a claim on the inheritance of Pedro the Cruel, and in the hope of making himself a ruler in Spain he went over seas with all the followers he could raise. He allied himself with his son-in-law, the King of Portugal, and at first conquered many towns in the northern provinces of Castile. But his army wasted away: the Castilians hated the memory of Don Pedro too much to submit to his heir, and after long struggles (1385–89) John was to return to England disappointed and grown old before his time.

During his absence Richard had reached the age of twenty, and at last assumed the governance of his realm. His chosen ministers were Michael de la Pole, and Robert de Vere, Earl of Oxford. The former was a man of a new family: his father had been a wealthy merchant of Hull, but he himself took to war and politics, rose to the front by his ability, and was now, in his middle age, made chancellor, and afterwards Earl of Suffolk. De Vere on the other hand held one of the oldest earldoms in England: he was a young man of the same age as the king, and had become his favourite companion. To raise him to a position above the rest of the barons Richard made him Marquis of Dublin and Duke of Ireland. After these two friends the king placed most confidence in his half-brothers (the sons of the Princess of Wales by her first marriage), Thomas Holland, Earl of Kent, and John Holland, who was afterwards made Earl of Huntingdon. *Richard's ministers.*

De la Pole and De Vere could not in any sense be called "favourites" in the objectionable sense of the term. The experience of one and the ancient nobility of the other made them persons whom it was quite fitting that the king should choose as his ministers. It may be that Michael was somewhat avaricious, and Robert somewhat vain and light-headed, but we have only their enemies' word for the accusation. Their rule was certainly no

[1] See page 68.

worse than that of their predecessors; the plot which was made against them must accordingly be attributed to jealousy and ambition, and not to patriotism. Thomas of Gloucester, who was set on holding the chief power under his nephew the king, drew into a conspiracy certain discontented nobles, the chief of whom were the Earls of Arundel, Warwick, and Nottingham, and the young Henry of Bolingbroke, the eldest son of the Duke of Lancaster.

In the Parliament of 1386 Gloucester and his friends made a great stir against the ministers, accusing them of embezzling the king's money, mismanaging the war with France (which still dragged on its weary length), and refusing to carry on the government according to the advice of the council and the two houses. De la Pole was impeached and declared guilty, though the accusations were wholly unfair. But the moment that the Parliament had dispersed the king gave him his pardon, and restored him to the office of chancellor.

This action of Richard's gave the conspirators the opportunity which they desired. At Gloucester's call they took arms and called out their retainers; marching on London they found no one to oppose them, and seized the town. They called themselves the "Lords Appellant", because they "appealed (accused) of treason" Suffolk, Oxford, and certain other of the king's advisers.

Rising of the Lords Appellant. Richard bade his followers take arms, and De Vere gathered some levies in the western counties. But at Radcot Bridge on the Upper Thames, near Lechlade, he was beset by a far greater host which the insurgent barons had sent out against him. After a brief skirmish the king's men surrendered, De Vere escaping with difficulty by swimming his horse across the river. He fled to France, where he was soon afterwards joined by De la Pole, who had also succeeded in getting away in safety from England. But the greater part of Richard's minor partisans did not leave the realm: they had not foreseen the merciless character of the Lords Appellant. Gloucester had determined to

THE LORDS APPELLANT.

break the spirit of the king, and to deal so harshly with his instruments that no man should ever dare to serve him again.

In February 1388 met the "Merciless Parliament", which was wholly dominated by the Lords Appellant, who had taken care to pack the Commons with their adherents. Gloucester behaved to his nephew with studied insolence: he brought out the documents which related to the deposition of Edward II., read them to the king before the assembly, and openly told him that there were good reasons for treating him as his great-grandfather had been treated. But for once he should be spared, and placed for the future in the hands of strong and wise counsellors. The Parliament then proceeded to impeach the king's ministers: Suffolk and Oxford had crossed the seas, so had Neville, archbishop of York, who also was cited as an offender. But there were at hand Tresilian, the chief justice, Sir Simon Burley, an old friend of the Black Prince who had been the king's tutor in his boyhood, and Nicholas Bramber, an ex-mayor of London, all prominent servants of the unfortunate Richard. After the mere mockery of a trial Tresilian and Bramber were hung, and Burley beheaded. Three knights of the king's household named Beauchamp, Berners, and Salisbury, were subsequently arrested, tried, and executed. The Parliament then voted liberal supplies for the expenses of government, from which the Lords Appellants were not ashamed to take £20,000 "to compensate them for the trouble and expense to which they had been put". Finally the king was made to renew his coronation oath before the Archbishop of Canterbury in St. Paul's cathedral, and after assisting at the ceremony the "Merciless Parliament" dispersed (June, 1388).

The Merciless Parliament.

CHAPTER VIII.

RICHARD II. 1388–1399.

The Lords Appellant were very much deceived if they imagined that their *coup d'état* was likely to reduce King Richard to a permanent state of dependence. He was no coward or trifler, and devoted the whole of the rest of his life to an elaborate scheme of vengeance against the men who had slain his friends and inflicted such deep humiliation on himself. Warned of the strength of Gloucester's party by the events of 1388, he was resolved to spend years, if necessary, in preparing for a new struggle: the next time he would have armed force at his back, and would not be caught unprepared.

The government of the Lords Appellant lasted no more than a year. It was not more fortunate or capable than that which it had superseded, for Gloucester soon showed that he was an intriguer and not a statesman. Nor was he even consistent in his policy: though he had always been an advocate of vigorous war with France, he now concluded a truce with the young King Charles VI. France was at the time in a condition not unlike that of England, for Charles was the victim of a tribe of domineering uncles, who dealt with him in much the same way that Lancaster and Gloucester dealt with Richard II. He made no objection to the long-needed suspension of hostilities.

In May 1389 King Richard found it possible to take the governance of the realm out of the hands of the Lords Appellants. He surprised those who were present at the council by suddenly asking his uncle, Gloucester, what was his own age. The duke answered that he was now in his twenty-third year. To this Richard replied that since he had so long passed his majority, he was old enough to govern his own realm, and that he would choose his own ministers. He formally thanked the Lords Appellants for their services, but said that he had

no further need for them. If he had dared to recall his
exiled friends, or to take open measures of vengeance against his oppressors, there is no doubt that civil war would have broken out. *Richard appoints new ministers.*
But Richard was now playing a very cautious game: he
made his grandfather's old advisers his ministers. The
good bishop William of Wykeham became chancellor,
and Brantingham of Exeter treasurer, just as they had
been in 1371. The Lords Appellants were not driven
out of the council, but allowed to keep their seats, though
they no longer dominated the whole body. Nothing was
done to which any exception could be taken, so the malcontents had no opportunity of appealing to the country
or rising in revolt.

The next eight years were by far the most fortunate
and prosperous part of King Richard's reign. He
governed well and wisely, and won golden opinions on
every side. The most statesmanlike of all his measures
was the conclusion of a permanent agreement with France.
The two countries were to be at peace for thirty years,
England retaining Calais and the district round Bordeaux
and Bayonne, but surrendering her claim to her other
lost possessions. The treaty was made firm by Richard's
marriage to Isabella, the eight-year-old daughter of the
French king. He had lately lost his first wife, Anne of
Bohemia, and so was free to wed again; but it was unwise to choose so young a bride, for *Peace with France.*
he had no children by his first marriage, and an heir to
the throne was much needed. As long as Richard was
childless his uncles and cousins were tempted to dream
of ultimately succeeding to his crown. As a temporary
measure of expediency he recognized as heir-apparent
Roger Earl of March, the grandson of Lionel of Clarence,
the second son of Edward III. (see table on p. 160). This
action was very ill-received by John of Gaunt and his son,
the Earl of Derby, who had secret hopes of asserting the
preference of the male to the female line of succession.

Among the most prominent features of the middle
years of Richard's reign was the growing importance of

the Wycliffites, or Lollards as they were now beginning to be called. The reaction which followed the Peasant Revolt had only checked their rise for a short time. The king himself neither identified himself with them, nor took any of the measures against them which the clergy endeavoured to press on him. His wife Anne had been distinctly favourable to them, and her foreign servants and followers took back to their native land the teachings of Wycliffe, which were destined to inspire John Huss, the great Bohemian reformer. Some of the baronage, among whom the Earl of Salisbury was the most prominent person, and a great number of the wealthier members of the citizen class were open supporters of the Wycliffite movement. The trend of the times was in their favour, for the Papacy was daily growing more scandalous. The "Great Schism" had now begun; and instead of one bad pope at Avignon, there were now two rival pontiffs, one at Avignon and one at Rome, who had excommunicated each other, and were endeavouring to stir up the states of Europe to a general religious war. Wycliffe's teaching had now become doctrinal as well as political. In his old age he had preached against the invocation of saints, the superstitious adoration of relics and images, the spiritual efficacy of pilgrimages, and the Real Presence in the Eucharist. He persisted in his old denunciation of the over-great wealth of the clergy, and the influence of his followers in the Parliament is shown by their repeated attempts to introduce legislation confiscating monastic lands and church endowments for the benefit of the state. Richard refused to countenance these proposals, but he was equally firm in refusing to allow the bishops to persecute the Lollards. Wycliffe has died in peace (1384), after having accomplished his great work of translating the Bible into the English tongue. His followers in the next generation were destined to fall upon more troublous times.

The Lollards.

Among other characteristic instances of King Richard's wise and careful governance of his realm may be mentioned his endeavour to introduce better order into Ireland, which his predecessors had systematically neglected for two hundred years. The English influence in the sister island had been greatly reduced during the reign of Edward II. by the repeated invasions of Edward Bruce, who had drawn many of the native septs into rebellion. The Scots were finally driven out, but the havoc they had wrought was never repaired, and the area over which the king's authority reached was permanently decreased. Many of the tribal chiefs of the north fell off from their allegiance, and, what was more dangerous still, many of the Anglo-Norman settlers drifted into close alliance with the rebels, adopted Celtic names, and "became more Irish than the Irish themselves". The assimilation of the new and the old inhabitants would have been advantageous both for themselves and for England if it had tended towards peace and union: but its sole effect was to increase tribal civil war and to diminish the central power of the government. Even the *Pale*, the district round Dublin which had been most thickly colonized by the English, began to fall into disorder. It was in vain that in 1366 King Edward III. caused the *Statute of Kilkenny* to be passed, forbidding the Anglo-Irish from mixing and marrying with the natives and adopting Celtic customs. Such laws can never be kept when the tendency of the times is against them, and the statute raised much bad blood between the settlers and the natives, without having any permanent effect in restoring the power of the king.

<small>State of Ireland.</small>

In 1394 Richard went over to Ireland to try the effect of his personal presence in setting the land in order: none of his predecessors since King John had visited it. His arrival was not without effect: many of the native chiefs did him homage, and the Lords of the Pale were for a space more obedient. He held a parliament of the whole land at Dublin, and then went home after appointing his heir-apparent, Roger Earl of March, Lord-Deputy of the island.

<small>Richard in Ireland.</small>

By 1396 Richard felt himself firmly established on the throne, and knew that he was liked and trusted by the majority of the nation. He felt that it would be no longer possible for a few powerful barons to rise against him and crush him as they had in 1388. Accordingly he thought that it was time for him to take in hand the punishment of his old enemies, the Lords Appellant. He had even gone to the pains of dividing them, by showing special favour to Thomas Mowbray the Earl of Nottingham, and Henry Earl of Derby, the two who had been least deeply implicated in the rising of 1388. His real enmity was directed against Gloucester, Arundel, and Warwick. It must be confessed that the duke gave his nephew every opportunity and provocation that he could have desired. He had intrigued against the French peace, insulted the king on his marriage, refused to keep the government of Ireland when it was given him, and caused his partisans in Parliament to make many perverse and unnecessary complaints against Richard's household and ministers. It was even said that he was plotting a second rebellion with the object of again seizing supreme power.

In 1397 Richard suddenly struck down his enemies. Warwick was arrested at a banquet, while Gloucester was captured by the king himself. He rode out to Plashy in Essex, the duke's favourite residence, and personally laid hands on him, telling him that he should "have the same mercy that he had shown to Burley nine years before". Arundel surrendered on promise of a fair trial before his peers. Richard then summoned a Parliament, and announced his intention of trying his three prisoners **Richard's** for treason. Copying their own procedure in **revenge.** 1388, he had them "appealed" by a number of the barons of his own party. Among the new "Lords Appellant" were included the king's half-brothers, Kent and Huntingdon, Mowbray Earl of Nottingham, Edmund of York, Earl of Rutland, and Scrope, a kinsman of the exiled Suffolk. Arundel and Warwick were duly impeached before their peers, both for their old doings and for the new treason laid to their charge. Both were condemned, and Arundel was beheaded, but Warwick's sentence was commuted to imprisonment for life in the Isle of Man. Gloucester did not appear for trial, but his death was reported to the Parliament. It seems clear that Richard had him secretly put to death in his prison at Calais, because he was determined not to spare him, yet shrank from the idea of ordering the public execution of such a near kinsman.

Thus the king had secured his long-deferred vengeance for the evil doings of the Merciless Parliament. He could not, however, recall his exiled friends Suffolk and Oxford, since both of them had died some time back. During the three years which he had yet to reign he did not delegate his authority to any ministers of such power and influence as De la Pole and De Vere, but carried out a purely personal government, using as his instruments men of no importance who could be trusted to obey his orders. The chief of them were Suffolk's kinsman Scrope, whom he made Earl of Wilts, and Bushey, the speaker of the House of Commons.

In this last period of his reign Richard displayed distinctly unconstitutional tendencies, which gradually estranged from him the popular sympathy which he had gained by his good governance between 1389 and 1396. His conduct was not yet exactly tyrannical, but it made men fear that he might some day grow more violent. He raised some "benevolences", or forced loans, from rich men whom he wished to keep in his dependence. He made persons whom he distrusted sign blank charters, which he could fill up at his pleasure with whatever terms he liked, if they should happen to displease him. Unlike the kings his predecessors, he always kept a large guard of archers about him. But most ominous of all was an innovation which he invented in the year 1398; he got Parliament to delegate its powers to a standing committee of ten peers, two bishops, and six commoners, whose consent to a statute or a tax was to have the same power as a parliamentary vote of approval. This was a most dangerous device, for it was obviously easy for the king

Richard's autocratic rule.

to dominate such a small body, and to wring from it the approval of things which the two houses themselves would not have been likely to grant. All these moves on Richard's part were menaces to the constitution, but he cannot be accused of having actually misgoverned the realm. He refrained from oppression, because he hoped to keep the people on his side. But he had already made enemies of a great part of the baronage, and of the clergy whom he had refused to aid in their attempts to attack the Lollards. The mass of the nation were not yet estranged from him, but they were seriously disturbed by his recent autocratic tendencies.

The actual cause of Richard's fall came from a matter of personal revenge. The two surviving Lords Appellant, Mowbray and Henry of Lancaster, fell into a quarrel, and accused each other of treason. Richard allowed them to challenge each other to a judicial duel; but when they appeared to fight it out in the lists at Coventry, he suddenly declared that the combat should not proceed, but that both should be banished the realm—Mowbray for life, Henry of Lancaster for ten years. This was regarded as a very hard decision, for one of the two must surely have been in the right. But there can be little doubt that Richard was merely carrying out to its final stage his vengeance for the acts of 1388. He had now punished all the murderers of Burley and Tresilian (1398).

Exile of Mowbray and Bolingbroke.

A year later John of Gaunt died at the age of sixty-one. The vast Lancaster estates and the ducal title fell to his banished son; but Richard very unjustly refused to hand them over to him, or to allow him to draw their revenues, taking them into his own possession. As Henry had not been declared a traitor, or properly convicted of any misdoing, there was obviously no justification for this action. It turned the exile into an open enemy, who was determined to risk anything to get revenge.

In 1399 his opportunity came. The Earl of March, the Lord-Deputy of Ireland, was slain in a skirmish by Irish rebels, and Richard hastily crossed to Ireland to restore order. He was engaged in a difficult campaign amongst the Wicklow mountains when he received the surprising news that Henry of Lancaster had landed at Ravenspur in Yorkshire, having in his company Archbishop Arundel, the brother of the deceased Lord Appellant, and a few other exiles. He proclaimed that he had only come to sue for his duchy of Lancaster, and had no treasonable designs (July, 1399). He was soon joined by thousands of the retainers of his father, and by many of the northern barons. The charge of the realm had been given during the king's absence to Edmund Duke of York, Richard's last surviving uncle, a simple and unenterprising old man. He gathered an army together, but foolishly disbanded it when Lancaster vowed that he had no treasonable design, and only wished to appeal to a free Parliament and to drive away evil councillors from the king.

Bolingbroke lands in England.

Thus Henry found himself unopposed, and had the realm at his feet, for Richard was detained at Dublin by persistent easterly winds which prevented him from crossing the Irish Channel. He soon showed the bent of his plans, by seizing and executing without fair trial the king's chief ministers, Scrope, Earl of Wiltshire, Bushey, and Green. This roused some of Richard's faithful adherents to take arms, and the Earl of Salisbury got together an army in Wales to meet his master on his expected arrival. But by an unlucky chance the weather still kept Richard storm-bound in Ireland, and he only reached Milford Haven two days after Salisbury's host had disbanded itself and gone home in despair.

Richard's ill-fortune.

The king had arrived almost alone, trusting to find his friends in arms and ready to aid him. He was soon surrounded by a force which Lancaster had sent against him, under Percy the Earl of Northumberland. On a false assurance sworn by the earl that nothing treasonable was designed against his crown or person, Richard surrendered himself. He was at once hurried up to London, where a Parliament had been hastily called together. Having now got his cousin into his hands, Henry showed that he aimed not at changing the ministry but at seizing the throne. The Parliament voted that Richard had forfeited his crown by breaking his coronation oath and governing unrighteously. On thirty-three separate charges, some of them absurd and all couched in exaggerated language, he was declared to have deserved deposition. Richard, much broken in spirit, yielded and consented to abdicate, whereupon his cousin stepped forward and laid claim to the crown. The deposed monarch was sent to Pontefract Castle, which he was never to leave alive.

<small>Richard deposed.</small>

CHAPTER IX.

HENRY IV. 1399-1413.

Down to the moment of his accession Henry of Lancaster had been aided by an extraordinary series of chances. The king's absence in Ireland, the feeble action of the Duke of York, the prolonged easterly winds which had kept Richard from returning to England, the supineness shown by his chief partisans, were circumstances on which Henry could not have counted when he landed at Ravenspur. If events had fallen out otherwise, it is probable that he would not have dared to seize the throne, but would have stopped short at his original programme of claiming justice for himself.

But the moment that the usurpation was complete the inherent weakness of the new ruler's position began to display itself. He was in reality no more than the king of a party; his only true supporters were the baronial faction which had been attached to the Lords Appellant, and the churchmen, headed by Archbishop Arundel, who had resolved to make him their instrument for the suppression of the Wycliffites. The support of other partisans could only be bought by encouraging a lively sense of favours to come. Meanwhile the deposed king had also a powerful baronial faction adhering to him, though for the moment it seemed crushed, and there were many parts of the country where his name was far more popular than that of Henry.

The house of Lancaster's claim to the crown was in truth dependent solely on the election by Parliament. In strict hereditary right the deposition of Richard II. made the young Earl of March (son of the Roger of March who fell in Ireland in 1398) heir to the throne. By setting him aside Henry committed himself to the theory of popular election to the crown, and he had, therefore, always to remember that Parliament might unmake him even as it had made him. Hence the most prominent characteristic of his domestic policy was a determination to keep the two houses in good temper at all costs, a line of conduct which often led him into a subservience to them which earlier kings would have regarded as degrading. Besides managing Parliament, Henry had to keep together the baronial party which supported him, and to grant the churchmen all that they asked.

Position of Henry IV.

Henry had been popular as Earl of Derby, but as king he found that he had no enthusiastic support from the nation. His enemies were many and active, his true friends were few, his interested supporters were greedy but lukewarm, while the bulk of the people cared little for him. It is a great proof of his ability that for fourteen years he kept tight hold on the crown, and finally passed it on to his son. His character was well suited for the task that he had undertaken; though unscrupulous, he was plausible, soft-spoken, and courteous; a proud or hot-tempered man would have ruined himself in a few years. But Henry was pliable, cautious, and wary, though when needful he could strike hard blows without hesitation.

He had only been two months on the throne when the first of the many rebellions with which he was to be plagued broke out. The leaders were, as might have been expected, the partisans of the late king—Richard's half-brother, John Holland, Earl of Huntingdon; his nephew, Thomas Holland, Earl of Kent; Montague, Earl of Salisbury, the best known of the Lollards; and Lord Despenser. Under cover of a tournament they collected several thousand armed men, and suddenly marched on Windsor, intending to catch the king unawares. Henry escaped by a lucky chance— he had only half an hour to spare—and fled to London, where he summoned the citizens to arms.

Rebellion of the Hollands.

The Hollands and their friends, finding that their first blow had failed, resolved to disperse in order to gather together greater forces: the main body began to retire westward, where they hoped to raise the numerous friends of King Richard in Wales and the Welsh border. This delay was their ruin: the king pursued them in haste, and they broke up without a pitched battle. Kent and Salisbury were slain in a skirmish at Cirencester, Huntingdon was caught and beheaded in Essex, Despenser at Bristol, both without any form of trial. Four minor chiefs were hung, drawn, and quartered in London. (Dec. 1399–Jan. 1400).

This ill-concerted rebellion caused the death of the unfortunate King Richard: to prevent further rebellion in his behalf Henry secretly caused him to be starved to death in Pontefract Castle. His agony is said to have endured fifteen days (Jan.–Feb. 1400). His corpse was publicly exposed, but the mystery of his death caused some people to believe that the body shown was not his, and for many years after rumours of his survival were current. An impostor who took his name lived all through Henry's reign at the court of Scotland.

Murder of Richard II.

The main event of note in the following year marks Henry's anxiety to secure his unsteady throne by giving guarantees for his fidelity to the church party. At the suggestion of Archbishop Arundel, he induced the Parliament to pass the infamous statute *De Heretico Comburendo*, which condemned to death by fire convicted heretics. No delay was made in commencing the persecution of the Lollards,

Persecution of the Lollards.

and before a month was out they counted their first martyr, William Sawtrey, a chaplain of London, who was burnt after steadfastly refusing to recant (Feb. 1401). The persecution went on intermittently for the next twenty years.

Though they obliged the king by countenancing his assault on the followers of Wycliffe, the Parliament took a very high tone with him in dealing with legislation and finance. They endeavoured to bind him down in the matter of expenses, and repeatedly propounded to him a theory that no grants of money ought to be made to the crown till all grievances petitioned against by the houses had been previously redressed. Henry temporized and procrastinated, putting off the evil day when he might be obliged to make this great constitutional concession.

Richard's death had some temporary effect in checking rebellions, for it was difficult to make the child Edmund of March the head of a political cause and to gather a party round his name. Moreover, the long uncertainty as to the deposed king's death kept men from recognizing his heir. The next troubles which Henry had to face were connected not with plots to change the English succession, but with a national rebellion in Wales. For a full century the principality had been undisturbed by civil strife, and Welsh troops had served Edward III. faithfully in all his wars. But now a chief of genius arose, in the person of Owen of Glyndwrdee, or Glendower, as the English called him, who descended from the old kings of Gwynedd. His countrymen Rebellion of Glendower. had never been partisans of Lancaster, and readily took arms when he called on them to resist the usurper. Owen made some pretence of rising in Richard's behalf, but he was really fighting for his own hand, to restore Welsh independence: the rebellion was national and had nothing to do with English dynastic matters. When Glendower descended from his hills it was not to rally partisans in England, but to ravage the border shires up to the gates of Shrewsbury and Worcester. Henry sent army after army against the rebels, but he could never catch them:

they retired to the mountains till the invader's food was exhausted, and turned to harass his rear-guard when he departed. When a larger expedition, led by the king himself, marched into Wales, it met with such bad weather and suffered so severely, that the English complained that Owen was a wizard and had leagued himself with the powers of the air to discomfit his foes (1402).

The Welsh rebellion gave no signs of spreading into England, but other troubles arose to touch Henry more nearly. The French king armed to avenge his dethroned son-in-law, and threatened invasion: Norman privateers ravaged many of the towns of the southern coast. At the same time the Scots, under the Earl of Douglas, crossed the Border and advanced into England. They suffered, however, a crushing defeat on Homildon Hill at the hands of Henry Percy, son of the Earl of Northumberland, and Douglas himself was taken prisoner with many other Scottish nobles (14th Sept., 1402).

This victory, however, was destined to have dangerous consequences. The king demanded that the captives should be made over to him, since he was desirous of filling his depleted exchequer with their ransoms. But the Percies had looked upon the money as their own, and bitterly resented the order. Northumberland had been Henry's chief supporter at his usurpation, and thought that nothing could be denied him. When peremptorily summoned to obey, he resolved to refuse, and hastily planned a rebellion, for his power was so great in the North that he could put into the field a whole army of his own retainers. The rising was a mere outburst of feudal anarchy, the Percy clan being its sole authors. Northumberland placed his gallant and reckless son Henry, whom men called Hotspur, at the head of his followers; he released his prisoner Douglas, who consented to espouse his cause, and he called in his brother Thomas Percy, Earl of Worcester, to his aid. They sent messengers to Owen Glendower to secure his co-operation, and resolved to use the name of the little Earl of March to cover their rebellion. They then for-

Rebellion of the Percies.

mally defied Henry, and declared him a perjured usurper and the murderer of his rightful king.

The elder Percy remained in Yorkshire to watch the loyalists of the north, who had taken arms under Ralph Neville, Earl of Westmoreland, the head of a family which had been the local rivals of the Percies. His son Henry ("Hotspur") and the Earls of Worcester and Douglas marched into Cheshire, a district always devoted to Richard II., and then pressed towards Shrewsbury, where Glendower and the Welsh were to join them. The king, however, marching hastily from London with a small army, threw himself between the Percies and Wales, and brought them to action at Hately field, two miles outside Shrewsbury. After a fierce battle Hotspur was slain, and his uncle and Douglas captured. Worcester was immediately beheaded: he deserved no better fate, as he had been one of those who betrayed Richard II., and had received more than £30,000 in gifts from the usurper against whom he now had taken arms (July 21, 1403). Northumberland, hearing that his son was dead, made abject professions of repentance, and was admitted to mercy on promising to surrender his numerous castles in the north. *Shrewsbury Field.*

Less than two years of comparative quiet followed the king's victory at Shrewsbury. Owen Glendower still held his own in Wales, but England was for a short time at peace. But in 1405 troubles began again: Henry's suspicions were first roused by an attempt to steal away the young Earl of March from Windsor, where he was kept in safe custody. Soon after insurrection again broke out in the north. It was directed by two leaders who had hereditary grudges against the king: Richard Scrope, Archbishop of York, was the brother of that Scrope Earl of Wilts who had been beheaded at Bristol in 1399; Thomas Mowbray, the Earl Marshal, was the son of the Mowbray whom Henry had accused of treason in 1398, and had faced in the lists of Coventry. His father had died in exile, and the son became a bitter enemy of the house of Lancaster. Scrope and Mowbray raised a force at York, and seeing rebellion afoot, the old Earl of Northumberland took arms in his own county to aid them. All three leaders agreed to recognize Edmund of March as king.

But Henry's fortune was still strong. His lieutenant the Earl of Westmoreland broke the back of the rising by capturing the Archbishop and the Earl Marshal by a villainous piece of ill faith. Having invited them to meet him under a flag of truce, he seized them when they came to the conference and put them in chains. Henry hurried northward, and on his arrival at York ordered both the prisoners to be executed. They received no trial before their peers, but were hurriedly condemned by an extemporized court, and beheaded an hour after (June 8, 1405). The death of Scrope caused wide-spread horror and dismay. No archbishop save Becket had ever been put to death for withstanding his king, and the northern clergy and people saluted Scrope as a martyr. Henry fell grievously ill a few days after, and was never a hale man for the rest of his life: the epileptic fits and leprosy which gradually grew upon him were universally regarded as Heaven's vengeance for the archbishop's cruel end.

Scrope's Rebellion.

But meanwhile the cause of rebellion did not prosper; the king's artillery blew Northumberland's castles to pieces in a few discharges, and the old earl had to flee into Scotland, where he lurked for three years, waiting for another opportunity for a blow at his enemy. Before it came, other troubles had been vexing Henry. His parliaments, with which he dared not quarrel, had learnt to treat him with scant respect. In 1406 they demanded and obtained from him the right to audit his accounts, and made him cut down the expenses of his household; in 1407 he had to acknowledge that the Commons had the sole right of initiating money grants. He was also made to promise to do nothing without first taking advice of his council. The weakness of his position is best understood by the fact that he allowed Parliament to deal with him in such a manner: no king whose throne was safe would have tolerated such interference.

In 1407 the foreign relations of the crown slightly improved. The danger of invasion from France had hitherto been very real: twice great French fleets had been collected in the Channel, and though they had not landed an army on the coast of Kent, yet flying squadrons had sacked many south-country ports, and once a considerable body of troops had been sent to aid Glendower in Wales. The soul of the opposition to Henry IV. had been Louis Duke of Orleans, the king's brother, but in November, 1407, he was murdered by the secret contrivance of his cousin, the Duke of Burgundy. His death was the cause of the outbreak of a long civil war between the party of nobles who had previously followed him and the partisans of Burgundy. Engrossed in domestic quarrels, the French had no longer any leisure to dream of invading England: their king, Charles VI., was utterly unable to keep his realm together, for he had become subject to fits of melancholy madness, which came on him every summer, and often disabled him for four and five months at a time. Soon, instead of France dreaming of molesting England, it was England which thought of interfering in faction-ridden France.

In 1408 Henry was able to suppress the last of the many insurrections which were raised against him. The old Earl of Northumberland, Lord Bardolf, and the Welsh bishop of Bangor slipped over the Border and raised a considerable force, but they were met and crushed at the battle of Bramham Moor by Sir Thomas Rokeby, sheriff of Yorkshire. Both the rebel peers were slain. This was the last trouble *Northumberland slain.* which came from the direction of Scotland, where King Henry had of late secured much influence over the government. For King Robert's son and heir, Prince James, was taken at sea as he was crossing to France (1406), and the Duke of Albany, who ruled in his brother's behalf, and wished to keep all the power for himself, made a secret agreement by which Henry undertook to hold the young prince a captive, while the duke covenanted in return not to molest England.

Thus Henry was freed from the danger on the side both of France and of Scotland, and had only the Welsh rebellion left on his hands. But he had fallen into wretched health, and from 1409 to 1411 was almost a chronic invalid. Most of the functions of government were discharged for him by his promising young son, Henry of Monmouth, the Prince of Wales. When only a boy he had fought at his father's side at Shrewsbury and in Wales; now as a young man of twenty he was already a hard-working statesman and soldier. There seems little room in his busy life for those curious tales of youthful riot and debauchery and consorting with disreputable companions which popular tradition associated with his name, and which the genius of Shakespeare has immortalized. The greater part of Henry's time was spent in hard soldiering in Wales, where he was constantly chasing Glendower's rebel bands, at first with small success. But as the years rolled on, the final triumph of the great guerilla chief grew less and less probable, since the house of Lancaster was growing more firmly established in England. At last his followers began to desert him, and Prince Henry was able to pacify the greater part of the country, though down to the day of his death Glendower was never wholly subdued.

Henry, Prince of Wales.

It is in the end of the period of Henry of Monmouth's administration in behalf of his father (Sept.–Dec., 1411) that the first English interference in France since the peace of 1393 falls. The quarrel of the Burgundian and Orleanist factions being at its height, Henry intervened in behalf of the former, and sent a small force across the Channel which helped the Burgundians to a victory over their enemies at St. Cloud. But this policy was not destined to be carried any further. In 1412 the king's health grew better for a short time, and he was able to take a greater share in public business. He seems to have somewhat resented the way in which his eldest son had monopolized the conduct of affairs during his illness, and showed his displeasure by relegating the Prince of

Wales to the background for a time, and employing his second son, Thomas Duke of Clarence, as his chief deputy and agent. In consequence of this change in policy, peace was made with the faction of Orleans, or the "Armagnacs" as they were now called, from their new leader, Bernard Count of Armagnac, who had taken the murdered duke's place.

Shortly after King Henry was once more smitten down with his old disease, and died rather suddenly at Westminster on March 20, 1413, after hav- *Death of the king.* ing been reconciled to his eldest son. After all his troubles and dangers he expired just as his throne seemed at last secure. But though he had rooted in his dynasty, his reign had not been a success. He left the country poorer than he had found it: civil war had been incessant, the central government was weak, the baronage and nation divided, and the blood feuds had been started that were to last for three generations, and to end in the terrible Wars of the Roses.

CHAPTER X.

HENRY V. 1413-1422.

The succession of Henry of Monmouth to his father's throne greatly strengthened the position of the house of Lancaster. The new king had gained the crown by quiet inheritance, not by armed force, and he was not responsible for the cruel death of Richard II. and the other crimes by which Henry IV. had climbed to power. Nor was he the man to imperil the position which he had obtained: he had been working hard both as warrior and as administrator since his early boyhood, and had received such a training as fell to the lot of none of his predecessors since Edward I. Though courteous and even-tempered, Henry could be stern on occasion: he was just according to his lights, but there can be no doubt that his views were often narrow and purely legal. His rigidly orthodox piety left no room in his heart for mercy to heretics. His most unjustifiable renewal of the French war and his persecution of the Lollards mark the unsympathetic side of his character. But he was well loved by the majority of his subjects: a ruler able, orderly, and conscientious, with a strong hand and an infinite capacity for work, was a great boon to the nation.

Henry's first acts after his accession were wise and graceful. He released the young Earl of March and restored him to his estates, though there was obviously some danger in setting at liberty a possible rival. He gave back the earldom of Nottingham to John Mowbray, brother of the Thomas Mowbray who had fallen with Scrope in 1405. He brought the body of Richard II. to London, and had it interred in state beside that of his wife, the "good Queen Anne". But soon after, Henry showed that one section of his subjects must expect no favour from him. He authorized Archbishop Arundel to proceed with greater vigour against the unfortunate Lollards. The most noted member of the sect was now Sir John Oldcastle, Lord Cobham, who had been an able and trusted lieutenant of the king during the Welsh wars. Oldcastle, when brought to trial, made a vigorous defence, denouncing the efficacy of penances and pilgrimages, the worship of images, the ambition and ill-living of the pope, and the greed of the friars. He was pronounced a heretic and sent back to the Tower, but escaped from it before the day fixed for his execution.

It seems that, in despair for their future, some of the Lollards now engaged in a plot to seize the king's person, and force him to take Oldcastle as his chief minister. It was their design to muster armed men in St. Martin's Fields by night, and make a sudden dash at the palace of Westminster. But the design was betrayed, and Henry, occupying the trysting-place beforehand, caught or scattered each band as it arrived. Nearly sixty Lollards were executed, the chief being a knight named Sir John Acton. But Oldcastle got away, and hid himself on the Welsh border. It was not till

Rising of the Lollards.

some years later that he was captured and executed as both heretic and traitor.

When once firmly set upon his throne King Henry proceeded to turn his attention to foreign politics. Like many other sovereigns in different epochs, he had formed the conclusion that the panacea for internal disorders is a successful war abroad. Nothing would strengthen the house of Lancaster more than a vigorous resumption of the old attacks on France, if only they could be carried to a fortunate conclusion. The state of affairs across the Channel seemed to promise an easy task for the invader: the Burgundian and Armagnac factions were waging open war upon each other throughout the land. The king was a hopeless lunatic; his son, the dauphin Louis, was a dissipated lad of seventeen, who had estranged half the people of the land by becoming a hot partisan of the Armagnacs. The prospect of a war with England was regarded with dismay by the French, and when Henry began to tamper with the Burgundians and to speak of renewing the old claims of Edward III., the dauphin's advisers seemed almost panic-stricken. Before a blow had been struck they offered the King of England the hand of the Princess Catherine, with a dowry of 800,000 crowns, and undertook to restore to him all those parts of Guienne and Gascony which had been lost by England since 1370. The duchy of Aquitaine, as constituted by the treaty of Bretigny, would have been brought back into being, save that Poitou and Saintonge were to remain French. *Henry's claim on France.*

But Henry was bent on war for war's sake, and had no intention of accepting these liberal offers. In 1415, after many months of negotiation, he broke off all relations with France, and began to make preparations for invading Normandy. No language can be too strong to use in the condemnation of his greed and ambition: for the political gain of the moment he condemned England and France to forty years of misery, and set on foot a war which was to prove the ruin of his own house.

In the summer of 1415 the army of invasion was mustered at Southampton: it was admirably equipped and composed of picked men, but its numbers were not large. Only 2500 men-at-arms and 7000 archers were assembled. They took with them the largest train of artillery that England had yet seen. The host was on the eve of sailing, when the kingdom was startled by the news that a dangerous conspiracy against the king's life had been discovered. It had been formed by Richard of York, Earl of Cambridge,[1] the king's cousin. He had married the sister of the Earl of March, and had planned to place his brother-in-law on the throne and rule under his name. March himself, a harmless and unenterprising young man, had no part in the plot: the chief accomplices of Cambridge were Lord Scrope, a kinsman of the archbishop who had been executed in 1405, and Sir Thomas Grey. They kept their counsel so ill that the king got wind of their designs, and arrested them before they were ready to strike. Full proof of their treason being produced, all three were executed (5 Aug., 1415). This plot was a purely dynastic business, the legitimate continuation of the many movements in favour of the house of March, which had disturbed the reign of Henry IV.

Plot of Richard of Cambridge.

In the middle of August the army crossed the Channel and landed near Harfleur, to which it laid siege. The place made a gallant resistance, but received no help from without, though the dauphin had mustered a large army at Rouen. The English suffered more from the summer heat and from camp fever than from the missiles of their enemies. After a siege of five weeks the artillery of the besiegers had so shaken the walls that the garrison surrendered (Sept. 22, 1415). A good foothold in Normandy had been secured, but meanwhile the season was growing late, and the army was dwindling away. When 1200 men had been told off to garrison Harfleur, and the numerous sick and wounded

Invasion of France.

---

[1] Second son of Edmund, Duke of York, who had been regent in 1399. His father was now dead, but his elder brother survived, and was holding the dukedom.

had been sent back to England, only 1000 men-at-arms and 4000 archers remained available for service in the field. This body was too small for a march on Paris or a serious attempt to subdue Normandy, and the king resolved to lead them across to Calais and not to advance deeper into France. Such a movement was rather a defiance of the dauphin and his host than a serious military movement. It would have been better to bring home the army by sea, for the march placed it in grave peril of destruction.

King Henry crossed Normandy and Picardy till he came to the Somme, which proved as great a barrier to him as it had been to Edward III. in 1346. He was only able to cross it by striking inland as far as Peronne; and while he was making this detour the French army, now commanded by John D'Albret, the Constable of France, outmarched him, and threw itself across his path. Close by the village of Agincourt the English found the way to Calais blocked by a host of six to eight times their own numbers. It was necessary at all costs to force a passage through them, for the weather had been bad, the army was worn out by long marches, and the provisions were almost exhausted. Accordingly Henry drew out his little force, and offered battle between the villages of Agincourt and Tramecourt (Oct. 25, 1415). He ranged his handful of men-at-arms in three small bodies, each flanked by two wings of archers, and waited to be attacked. The ground between him and the French was rain-sodden ploughed fields, by no means easy to cross when the knightly armour had grown so heavy that it was no longer a simple matter to march in it. The French, despising the small numbers of their enemies, thought that an easy victory was in their hands. They sent before them, as at Poictiers, two squadrons of mounted men, who were to break in upon the flanks and rout the archers, while the main body followed on foot in three dense lines, each larger than the whole English army (25 Oct., 1415).

The cavalry in advance struggled through the heavy

ground till they came in range of the archery, when they were shot down almost to a man without striking a blow. The masses of dismounted knights lurched heavily on in their wake, but were brought to a stand by their fatigue, and by the deep clay, in which they sank almost to their

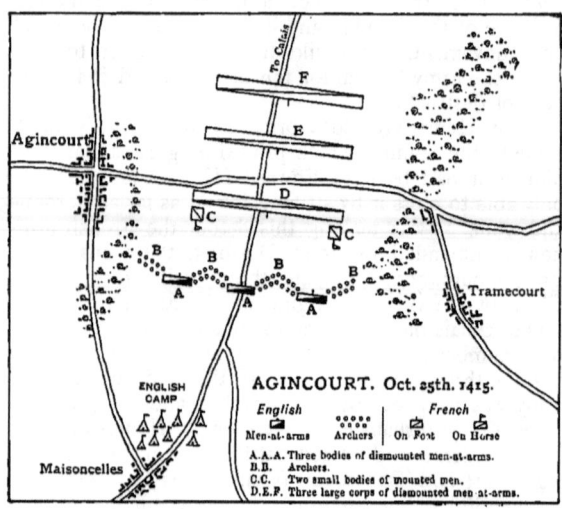

knees. They halted in exhaustion some distance in front of the English line. Seeing their plight, King Henry made his men advance, and pausing at a convenient distance from the mass bade his bowmen let fly into it for some minutes, and then to close. The French line of battle, already riddled by the arrow-shower, was easily routed by the impact of the charge: the knights were rolled helplessly into heaps, and slain or made prisoners by the lightly-armed bowmen, who proved far more effective than the men-at-arms on such ground. The moment that the first line was disposed of, Henry pushed on against the second, which made a somewhat better resistance, but was finally broken up and slaughtered like

Battle of Agincourt.

the first. The third line melted from the field without fighting, save a few of its chiefs, who refused to fly, and went forward to certain death. While they were being disposed of, an alarm was raised that the English camp was being attacked from the rear, and the king ordered his men to slay their captives, and turn back for a new fight. But the diversion was caused only by bands of marauders, who fled when they saw the king moving upon them, so that the slaughter of the prisoners, which had been begun, proved wholly unnecessary, and was stopped. When the field was searched by the victors, they found among the slain the Constable and three dukes, Brabant, Bar, and Alençon, with seven counts, ninety barons, and five or six thousand men-at-arms, numbers greater than these of the whole English army. Fifteen hundred prisoners of rank still survived, among them the young Duke of Orleans and the Counts of Vendôme, Eu, and Richemont.

The English loss was trifling; though two great peers had fallen, Edmund, Duke of York, and Michael, Earl of Suffolk, only thirteen men-at-arms and a hundred archers had perished with them. The heavy armour of the French seems to have been as fatal to their power of striking effective blows as to their ability to move in the sodden plough-land. The arrows pierced their mail with ease, while in the close fighting they seem to have been at an equal disadvantage, and were dashed down helplessly by the axes and maces wielded by the bare arms of the archers. The victory seemed to justify Henry's rash march across France, and in the actual fighting his tactical skill had been as evident as his personal courage; but if the French had been commanded by a cautious and capable general it is hard to see how he could have escaped a disastrous defeat.

Henry's army was so small and so exhausted that he could make no immediate use of the victory, and was obliged to march on to Calais and thence take ship to London. He was received with a splendid triumphal procession, but his victory had been more showy than fruitful, and the possession of Harfleur was the only tangible benefit which had resulted from his campaign. The Armagnac party had not been crushed, even by the carnage at Agincourt, and there was some fear that the Burgundians might be driven into opposing England by a tardy revival of patriotic spirit. Harfleur was beset by the French for the whole of the next year, and had a narrow escape of falling back into their hands.

For the greater part of 1416 Henry was busied with negotiations with the Emperor Sigismund, who visited England, full of great plans for restoring peace to Christendom by putting an end to the "Great Schism" which had been rending the church in twain since 1378. Henry gladly lent himself to this scheme, which had taken shape at the Council of Constance. Two popes having been deposed and a third forced to resign, a universally acknowledged pontiff was secured in the person of Martin V. (1417). But the council is better remembered for the burning of John Huss, the great Bohemian reformer and the spiritual heir of Wycliffe, than for its abortive attempt to reform the debased papacy. In return for Henry's assistance in matters ecclesiastical, Sigismund endeavoured to negotiate a peace with France on terms favourable to England. But the Armagnacs would not listen to the exorbitant claims of the victor of Agincourt, and the Burgundian duke held aloof, willing to profit by his enemies' misfortunes but afraid to offend the national spirit of France by an open alliance with England. The war had therefore to continue.

Raising an army of about the same size as that of 1415, the king crossed the sea in August, 1417, and began to overrun Normandy. This time he came not to execute a plundering raid, but to conquer the land piecemeal: one after the other he took Caen, Lisieux, Bayeux, Alençon, and Mortaigne, cutting a huge cantle out of the duchy, in which he established a solid base for further operations. The Armagnacs and Burgundians were fighting hard round Paris, and paid no attention to the invader. In the next year he steadily pushed his sphere of operations to right and left, conquering St. Lô, Coutances and Cherbourg in the west, and then turning east to lay siege to the great city of Rouen. He kept stern discipline among his troops, and gave such good government to the conquered districts that it contrasted strongly with the anarchy which had prevailed before. Meanwhile the struggle at Paris had ended in success for the Duke of Burgundy: the populace had risen against his rivals, massacred the Constable Armagnac with many of his party, and driven the rest away. The duke became by his victory responsible for the conduct of the war with England, but shewed himself as incapable as the Constable had been of checking King Henry. By allowing the gallant defenders of Rouen to remain unsuccoured for six months he drew down upon himself the condemnation of every patriotic Frenchman. In January, 1419, the Norman capital fell, reduced by sheer famine, and Henry entered its gates. Then at last did John of Burgundy begin to stir, but it was not in order to raise against the English the whole force of France, but to make one last attempt to buy them off by offering more liberal terms than the Armagnacs had proffered. But a conference at Meulan (May, 1419) revealed that Henry's terms were as exorbitant as ever; he asked for all the lands granted to Edward III. by the treaty of Bretigny, and the whole duchy of Normandy, as well as for the arrears of King John's long unpaid ransom-money of 1360. In despair at the arrogant demands of the English king, Burgundy resolved to make peace with the Armagnac faction, and unite with them for a last desperate attempt to expel the invader. His enemies were now headed by Charles, the youngest son of the mad king, who had become dauphin on the death of his elder brothers. They professed their readiness to come to terms with the Burgundians, but when the two princes met in conference on the bridge of Montereau (10th September, 1419), the dauphin's attendants treacherously fell upon the duke and hewed him down as he knelt before his cousin.

This brutal and senseless murder had the natural result: the duke's young son, Philip, and all the partisans of Burgundy, at once went over to the English side, and swore that Charles should never reign over France. Rather than acknowledge the murderer as heir to the throne, they would accept Henry's ill-founded claim and take him as their ruler. All the cities of northern France, where the Burgundians were strong, thus became friendly to the English, and opened their gates to the invader. On May 20, 1420, Henry entered Troyes with the young duke Philip at his right hand, and there met the Queen of France, her insane spouse, and her daughter Catharine, whose hand had been offered to him as far back as 1414. The unfortunate Charles VI. was made to give his consent to a treaty by which he made Henry regent of France, and gave him the right of succession to the throne on his own death, to the exclusion of the dauphin. On June 2 the English king married the Princess Catharine, in order to give himself some better claim to the crown than the mad king's bequest. After turning his arms against those towns in the neighbourhood which still held out for the Armagnacs, and reducing them, Henry brought his bride and his father-in-law to Paris, where he celebrated his Christmas festivities in great state.

Treaty of Troyes.

Early in the spring he returned to England, and made a progress round the whole land with his wife, to receive the homage and congratulations of his admiring subjects. No king of England had ever wrought such feats of arms, and it seemed that he had carried to a successful end the great war which had cost his predecessors so much fruitless expense of life and wealth. Parliament ratified all the provisions of the Treaty of Troyes with alacrity, not noting, we may suspect, the danger which accompanied it that England might ere long become a mere province of France, "for the greater ever draws the less". But it was not long before a jarring note was struck to mar the

DEATH OF HENRY V.

universal harmony. In April, 1422, news came to England of a disaster on the Loire. The king had sent his eldest brother, Thomas Duke of Clarence, to chase the Dauphinois out of Anjou and Maine, but the enemy had received a large reinforcement from Scotland under the Earl of Buchan, and for the first time since Agincourt turned to fight in the open. *Battle of Baugé.* Recklessly pursuing, with his archers far to the rear, Clarence ran into an ambush at Baugé (March 21, 1422), and was there surrounded and slain; his companions, the Earls of Somerset and Huntingdon, were taken prisoners.

The news of this defeat soon drew the king back to France (June, 1422). He marched south and drove the Dauphinois back to Orleans and beyond the Loire, then he turned to reduce their few remaining strongholds in central France. None of them gave him much trouble, save Meaux, whose garrison made a resistance of unparalleled obstinacy. Henry formed the siege in October, and the town did not yield till May; *Siege of Meaux.* all through a winter of perpetual rain he lay before its walls, obstinately refusing to draw back from his flooded trenches. He and his army were smitten with a terrible plague of ague and dysentery, which thinned their ranks even faster than starvation diminished those of the garrison. When spring came the town yielded, and Henry, showing the stern cruelty which not unfrequently disfigured his action, hung the governor and four of his companions. He then turned back towards Paris, and ere long his wife, and the infant son whom she had lately borne him, rejoined him. But men saw that he was no longer himself: the hand of death *The king's death.* was upon him, for the chills of his winter camp had stricken him with an exhaustion from which he could not rally. He took to his bed in the castle of Vincennes, near Paris, and lingering in a state of utter prostration through the summer heat, died on August 31, 1422, leaving all his great conquests to a weakly child of less than a year old.

CHAPTER XI.

HENRY VI. THE MINORITY AND THE FRENCH WAR.
1422-1450.

The death of Henry V. was followed in a few weeks by that of his imbecile father-in-law Charles VI. (Oct. 21); thus the crowns of England and France both fell, according to the provisions of the Treaty of Troyes, to the sickly child, Henry of Windsor. It might have been expected that the domination of the English across the Channel would disappear when the strong personality of the conqueror was removed, and the power which he had wielded passed into many hands. But the Dauphin Charles, the "King of Bourges" as men now called him, was both unpopular and apathetic; his councillors and captains were incapable, and they could make no profit out of the opportunity which was offered them. As long as the young Duke of Burgundy remembered his father's murder and remained the ally of the English, the nationalist party was unable to make any head against the invaders.

Henry V. had left two surviving brothers: John Duke of Bedford, the elder of the pair, was made regent of France, an office which he discharged with great energy and ability, doing his best to carry on the war with very inadequate resources, and conciliating Philip of Burgundy to the best of his power. To bind him yet more closely to the English alliance, John wedded the duke's sister, the Princess Anne. Humphrey of Gloucester was a very different character from his steady and hard-working brother: he was flighty, petulant, quarrelsome, and selfish, though his affable manners, his patronage of learned men, and his cultivation of all the arts of popularity won him the name of "the good Duke Humphrey" from his numerous partisans. Gloucester had been regent of England at his brother's death, but the Lords of the Council and the Parliament feared his reckless ambition so much that they would only allow him to con-

Bedford and Gloucester.

tinue in power under many restrictions. Instead of Regent they made him only "Protector of the Realm and the King's Chief Councillor", and he was to act in all things with the consent of a Council of Regency composed of fifteen members. The chief opponent of the duke was his half-uncle Henry Beaufort, Bishop of Winchester, an able and obstinate man, who thoroughly distrusted his nephew: the majority of the council generally backed the bishop, and Gloucester spent much of his time in fruitless bickerings with them.

It is most astonishing to find that the death of Henry V. was not followed by any shrinkage of the English possessions in northern France. On the contrary, the area of the region which acknowledged his little son as king continued slowly to increase for more than six years. Bedford was zealous and untiring in his exertions, and though help was doled out to him from England with a very sparing hand, he contrived to keep up the war—to a great extent by the use of French money and French mercenaries. Twice the Dauphinois strove to break into the provinces of the English obedience, but they suffered two bloody defeats at Cravant (July 31, 1423) and Verneuil (Aug. 17, 1424). In the second of these fights fell the Earl of Douglas and nearly all the Dauphin's Scottish auxiliaries. Further aid from Scotland was hard to get, for the English government had just released and restored to his kingdom the long-imprisoned King James I. That prince had married an English wife, Joan Beaufort, the bishop's niece, and adopted a policy of consistent friendliness to his southern neighbours. *Successes in France.*

The first danger to the English dominion in France came from a freak of Humphrey of Gloucester. He provoked the Duke of Burgundy to great wrath by marrying Philip's cousin Jacquelaine, Countess of Holland and Hainault, who had absconded from her lawful husband, the Duke of Brabant. Obtaining for her a divorce of more than doubtful validity from the Anti-pope Benedict XIII., the duke wedded her, and tried to make himself master of her heritage in Hainault. *Jacquelaine of Holland.*

Burgundy had no desire to see Gloucester established as a neighbour to his county of Flanders, and joined John of Brabant in overrunning Hainault. He might even have broken away from the English alliance if he had not been turned aside by the soft words of his brother-in-law Bedford. Gloucester meanwhile proved himself an indifferent champion of his wife's claims: he fled back to England, while she fell into the hands of Duke Philip, and was thrown into prison. Instead of pursuing the quarrel further, Humphrey very meanly acknowledged that his marriage had been invalid, and consoled himself by marrying Eleanor Cobham, a Kentish lady who had taken his fickle fancy (1427).

After escaping the dangers to which his reckless brother's conduct had exposed him, Bedford was ere long to be confronted by a far more formidable difficulty. Slowly pushing his operations southward he arrived at the gates of Orleans, the last French stronghold north of the Loire. To besiege this important strategical point the whole available field-army of the Regent was sent forward under the Earl of Salisbury—the son of Richard II.'s Lollard friend. So limited, however, were the resources of the English that the expedition did not exceed 4000 men. Yet weak as was the attack, the defence was weaker still, and Salisbury was able to blockade the place by erecting a number of forts (*bastilles* as they were called) watching all its gates: he was unable with his inadequate numbers to erect a complete line of circumvallation. The French made several feeble attempts to save Orleans, of which the best known was that foiled at the "Battle of the Herrings". A small reinforcement from Paris, guarding a convoy largely composed of salt fish "and other Lenten stuff", was attacked near Rouvray by the Dauphin's forces, but parked its wagons in a square and easily beat off the French by the force of archery (Feb. 12, 1429). Nevertheless Orleans held out stoutly, and Salisbury soon after was killed by a cannon-ball as he was reconnoitring its walls.

Siege of Orleans.

After the "Battle of the Herrings" Charles seemed to

THE MAID OF ORLEANS. 119

have resigned himself to the prospect of losing Orleans: but in the early spring of 1429 a new factor appeared in the war, and the fortune of the English at last began to wane. Patriotic hearts all over France were deeply stirred by the fact that for fifteen years a foreign enemy had been able to overrun and plunder the whole land, owing to the bitter civil strife which divided its inhabitants into two hostile camps. The English were insignificant in numbers, and could not for a moment have maintained themselves, but for the fact that a disloyal French faction gave them active aid, while the apathetic majority stood aside and allowed the Dauphinois and the Burgundians to fight out their disreputable blood-feud to a miserable end. Meanwhile the country-side lay desolate, the towns were sinking into decay, and the land groaned for a deliverer from the interminable war. Help came from an unexpected quarter: Jeanne D'Arc, a young country girl from Domrémy on the borders of Lorraine, had been from her youth a dreamer of dreams and a seer of visions. While her mind was brooding over the misery of her country she was visited by a series of ecstatic trances in which she believed that her patron saints, the Virgin, St. Michael, and St. Catharine, appeared to her and bade her save France by preaching unity to all Frenchmen, and setting them an example of vigorous action. After some doubting she set out to seek the Dauphin's court at Chinon, and presented herself before the apathetic prince, bidding him bestir himself and drive out the English by means of the divine aid which she brought him. Her visions promised her that she should relieve Orleans and lead Charles to Rheims, there to crown him king. Convinced by some secret token which Jeanne revealed to him, or perhaps moved only by motives of policy, the Dauphin gave his sanction to her mission, and sent her forth with an expedition which was about to attempt to succour the beleaguered garrison of Orleans. She assumed knightly armour, girt on a sword which was said to have been discovered by a miracle in the church of St. Catharine at Fierbois, and bore a white

Joan of Arc.

banner. The French leaders were at first inclined to treat her as a mere impostor or fanatic, but the soldiery eagerly accepted her as an emissary of Heaven, and went forth with a confidence which they had not shown since Agincourt. She entered Orleans in safety (April 30), and then led a series of sorties against the English forts which lay around it, heading the storming parties in person. Such was the enthusiasm with which the garrison followed her that her enterprises were successful, and the besiegers, seeing their line broken, were compelled to raise the leaguer and retire into their nearest strongholds, Jargeau and Beaugency. Rapidly following them up, Jeanne captured both places, and then defeated in the open field at Patay (June 18) the wrecks of the beaten army strengthened by a reinforcement from Paris under Lord Talbot.

Joan relieves Orleans.

This series of astonishing successes gave the French the confidence which they had so long lacked, while the English, amazed at defeats which they could not understand, declared that Jeanne was a witch and an emissary of the devil. "Before her day", wrote a contemporary chronicler, "two hundred English would drive five hundred French before them; but now two hundred French would beat and chase four hundred English." For the future the offensive was always taken by the Dauphin's troops, and the invaders would only fight on the defensive.

After the victory of Patay the Maid escorted Charles to Rheims, as she had promised, and there saw him crowned King of France (July 17, 1429). After this triumph she begged leave to withdraw home, but her presence was considered too valuable, and she was begged to stay with the army. Yielding to the request, she then advised an instant attack on Paris: it was carried out, but with such slackness and mismanagement that it failed. Jeanne herself was wounded as she urged on the troops to the storm, and her prestige suffered somewhat from the repulse. But meanwhile Senlis, Beauvais, Laon, and Soissons surrendered to the new king, and as a result of Jeanne's appearance all Champagne and most of the Isle de France had been abandoned by the English: even their hold on Paris and Normandy had been shaken.

Next spring the Maid again took the field, though her ungrateful master sent her forth with a very inadequate force at her back. She declared herself that her career was nearing its end, but persevered gallantly in the task which she had undertaken. After some small successes she threw herself into Compiégne, which was being beleaguered by a Burgundian army. Leading a sally of the garrison to beat up the besiegers' camp, she was unhorsed and taken prisoner. Philip of Burgundy sold her to the English for 10,000 crowns, and she was led into captivity. The Regent Bedford was always reckoned a just and wise prince, but in this case he shamefully belied his reputation: he had no mercy for "the limb of the devil", as he called the unfortunate Jeanne. She was for some time held in bonds, and subjected to cruel maltreatment in order to induce her to declare that her mission was not from God. Persevering in her belief to the end, she shamed her keepers by her courage and piety. At last Bedford commissioned the Bishop of Beauvais to proceed against her as a witch. After a formal trial before a French ecclesiastical court she was condemned and burnt to ashes at Rouen on May 30, 1431. Charles VII. was only less guilty than the English in this black business: he made no effort whatever to rescue his saviour, though he had in his hands Lord Talbot and many other English prisoners, and could have stopped Jeanne's persecution at any moment by threatening to retaliate on his captives any judgment that might be passed on her.

Martyrdom of Joan of Arc.

The Maid died unavenged, but the movement which she had set on foot did not die with her. She had destroyed the self-confidence which had made the English almost invincible. She had also stirred up the heart of the French nation, and taught them to forget their wretched factions and feuds. From the moment of her appearance the Burgundian partisans of the English began one by one to drop off, and to make their peace with Charles VII. In spite of all his faults they saw that he represented the cause of French independence, and that it was a sin to fight against him in the ranks of the invader. Bedford did his best to struggle against fate, and his military talents availed for some years to stem the tide, but he felt himself that he was only postponing the inevitable. The fatal blow was struck when at last Philip of Burgundy consented to forget his father's murder, and The Peace to make peace with the murderer. At the of Arras. Congress of Arras he threw up his long alliance with England, and reconciled himself to Charles (Sept. 10, 1435). Four days later the Regent John of Bedford died at Rouen, worn out by his long campaigning. For twelve years he had hardly been given a moment's rest, and he saw that the ruin of the cause which he had so long maintained was at hand.

Bedford had not been buried seven months when Paris, the last refuge of the English in central France, fell into the hands of the enemy. The burghers, once such hot partisans of Burgundy and England, opened the gates to the besiegers, and Lord Willoughby with his small garrison had to fly in haste (April, 1436). Nothing was now left to the English but their old foothold in the duchy of Guienne, around the ever-loyal Bordeaux, and in the north Normandy and part of Maine. It is therefore most extraordinary to find that in these limited regions they were able to maintain themselves for no less than sixteen years more.

The chief heroes of this last and most hopeless stage of the Hundred Years' War were John Lord Talbot, and Richard Duke of York. The latter was the son of that Richard Earl of Cambridge who had conspired against Henry V. in 1415. He had succeeded to the duchy of York when a young boy on the death of his childless uncle, Duke Edmund, at Agincourt. But he became a much more important personage in 1425, when his other uncle, Edmund Mortimer Earl of March, died, and left him his heir. Through his mother Anne Mortimer, Richard now represented the eldest line of Edward III.'s descendants. He was twice appointed to the command in France, and held it from 1435 to 1437, and again from 1441 to 1445. He kept a tight hold on Normandy, beating off assault after assault upon the duchy, and often pushing raids almost to the gates of Paris. He even recovered from the French in 1437 the important fortress of Pontoise, one of the keys of the Seine, and it was maintained till 1441, being four times relieved and reprovisioned by the indefatigable Talbot. When York was recalled from France in 1445, and replaced by Edmund Beaufort, Duke of Somerset, a commander of a much lower stamp, the power of resistance of the English in Normandy seemed to collapse, and place after place began to fall into the hands of the enemy.

Richard of York.

Meanwhile the internal affairs of England present little that is of importance. A long struggle went on between Humphrey of Gloucester, representing the extreme war party, and Beaufort, now a Cardinal, who led those who were in favour of coming to an agreement with France, and sacrificing the untenable claim to the French throne in return for some territorial concessions. Gloucester gradually lost ground, more especially after 1441, when his wife, Eleanor Cobham, was prosecuted for using sorcery to compass the king's death, and rightly or wrongly condemned to imprisonment for life. Her husband made no attempt to defend her, but whether from cowardice, or from consciousness that she was guilty, it is impossible to tell.

The temporary discredit of the war party led to serious negotiations with France in 1444. The king had now attained his majority, and men trusted that a new era would commence when he took over the conduct of affairs from the hands of the council. He himself was set on peace, and it was hoped that the agreement might be sealed by his marriage with a French princess. Unfortunately, however, the son of the heroic Henry V., and the grandson of the politic Henry IV., turned out to be the weakest sovereign that ever sat upon the English throne. A gentle, pious, in-

The Truce of Tours.

capable young man, he was full of good wishes, but lacked the strength to put them into practice. He was so modest and diffident that he was always ready to defer to the opinion of the nearest adviser; but the next person that had his ear could as easily turn him from his first purpose. One unfortunate heritage from his ancestors showed itself in him long ere he reached middle age—a touch of the melancholy madness of his grandfather, Charles VI. of France. When it fell upon him he had to be placed in retirement, and the cloud did not pass from his brain for many months. He was entirely well meaning, and his people loved his pious and simple character, but they were at the same time driven to despair by the hopeless incapacity which he showed for affairs of state. Usually he was merely the mouthpiece of those behind the throne.

Character of Henry VI.

The full extent of Henry's weakness was not yet known, when in 1444 he allowed his minister, William de la Pole, Earl of Suffolk, a partisan of Cardinal Beaufort, to sign the Truce of Tours. By this agreement the English retained their foothold about Bordeaux and in the duchy of Normandy, but gave up their fortresses in Maine and other outlying regions. At the same time the king received the hand of Margaret of Anjou, a cousin of Charles VII., daughter of Réné, Duke of Anjou and titular King of Naples. The terms which Suffolk had obtained were very unfavourable; in return for the ceded strongholds, England should have got something more than an uncertain truce and a dowerless bride for her king.

When the details of the Truce of Tours were divulged, Gloucester again raised his head and began to clamour against the cession of Maine. He found plenty of support from the enemies of Suffolk and the Beauforts, and was able to make himself most unpleasant to the young queen. Margaret was a woman of strong passions and considerable ability, who soon learned how to domineer over her meek husband, and was quite reckless in using her power. She threw herself vehemently into English politics as an enemy of Gloucester and his party, and started her career in England as the leader of a faction. At the Parliament of Bury (Feb. 1447), she and Suffolk concocted a *coup d'état* against Humphrey. He was seized and thrown into prison, where he at once died: there were strong suspicions of foul play, but it seems more likely that apoplexy, caused by a fit of passion, carried off the Duke. His old rival Cardinal Beaufort, who had retired from politics a few years before, only survived him for five weeks.

Death of Duke Humphrey.

The government of the realm now passed for a space into the hands of Suffolk, the Queen, and Edmund Beaufort, Duke of Somerset, who used the king's name at their pleasure. The leadership of the opposition, on the other hand, had devolved on Richard Duke of York, a far more able man than Duke Humphrey; he had never forgiven the way in which his career in Normandy had been brought to an end by his being superseded by Somerset. At all costs the ministry should have endeavoured to turn the truce with France into a permanent peace. But they were unable to do so, and, what was worse, could not keep their own troops in Normandy in order. A disgraceful raid into Brittany by some mutinous bands, whom Somerset had left unpaid, gave the French an excuse for renewing the war (March, 1449).

The best testimony to the incapacity of the English government was the extraordinary rapidity with which Normandy was lost. In less than a year Somerset had been driven out of the duchy which York and Talbot had so long maintained against all the strength of France. A small army of relief, sent over from Southampton, was cut to pieces at the battle of Formigny (April 15, 1450), and four months later Cherbourg, the last fortress held for England, lowered its flag. Nothing now remained to England in northern France save the single stronghold of Calais.

The loss of Normandy.

The outburst of wrath which followed Somerset's disgraceful loss of Normandy marks the opening of a new period in English history. Civil strife was about to be added to foreign war, and the Wars of the Roses were close at hand.

CHAPTER XII.

THE WARS OF THE ROSES. 1450-1464.

Down to the moment of the loss of Normandy the misfortunes of the French war had provoked no more than a certain amount of clamorous criticism of the king's ministers. The burden of the war had not been very heavily felt; it had been largely maintained with French money, and the parliamentary grants in aid had not been extravagant. The drain of men had been considerable, but it had fallen entirely on volunteers and mercenaries. The hope of conquering all France had long been abandoned, and as long as a broad foothold was kept beyond the Channel, the details of the struggle had not been minutely investigated. It was generally thought that a good deal of mismanagement and maladministration was going on, and grumbling never ceased, but there had as yet been no great explosion of popular wrath. The fact that the opposition was headed by a discredited and reckless busybody like Humphrey of Gloucester had also availed somewhat to weaken its criticism of the ministers.

Now, however, matters were changed. The great Duchy of Normandy had been lost in a few months, and this disaster fell like a thunder-clap on the nation. Moreover, the discontented had now got an able and popular leader in Richard of York, who (as men now began to remember) was very near the throne. Since Gloucester's death the duke was the first prince of the blood, and the king's nearest kinsman. Moreover, Henry had now been five years wedded and yet had no offspring: if he continued childless, Richard would inherit his crown. For this reason both York himself and his admirers were much incensed that, in spite of his well-known ability, he was excluded as far as possible from

Richard of York.

public affairs; indeed he had of late been sent into a kind of honourable banishment by being made Lord-deputy of Ireland (1448) for a term of ten years. In the unhappy sister-island he proved to be one of the few successful governors whom England has entrusted with the unenviable post. He and his house were ever after very popular in Ireland.

Nor was Richard powerful by reason of his popularity alone: his following among the baronage was very considerable. He himself, through his father's marriage with Anne Mortimer, sister of the last Earl of March, was one of the greatest landholders in the realm. He had wedded Cicely Neville, a daughter of the greatest baronial house in the England of that day. Her brother Richard Neville Earl of Salisbury, and her nephew Richard Neville Earl of Warwick[1] (the famous "king-maker" of a later day) were always the trusty partisans of the duke. Three other Neville peers, the Lords Abergavenny, Latimer, and Fauconberg, firmly adhered to the family politics of their race. Another faithful friend was John Mowbray, Duke of Norfolk: he was the nephew of York's wife Cicely Neville, but his opposition to the king's ministers was probably due rather to an ancient blood-feud with the house of Lancaster; for his uncle was the Mowbray who had been beheaded at York in 1405, and his grandfather was the unfortunate opponent of Henry IV. in the lists at Coventry. Three or four other houses of minor note were allied with the Nevilles and Mowbrays, and the whole group constituted a faction of formidable strength. The baronage of England had been dwindling in numbers for a century and more: there were now not more than thirty or forty lay peers in the House of Lords. Each of the titles of the year 1450 represented three or four of the old baronies of the time of the Edwards. Hence a compact group of a dozen peers now comprised a third of the whole baronage of England. The estates

The Nevilles.

[1] The elder Neville had married Alice, heiress of Salisbury, granddaughter of the Lollard earl who fell in 1400. The younger Richard had wedded Anne, heiress of Warwick, and had obtained her great heritage in the western Midlands and on the south Welsh border.

of Mortimer, Mowbray, and Neville were scattered thickly all over England, and gave rallying points in almost every county for the partisans of York.

There is no proof whatever that Duke Richard had personally dabbled in treasonable schemes before he had been banished to Ireland by the king's ministers. His conduct all through Henry's minority had been loyal and correct. It seems that he was first roused to action by the clamours of the nation, and only moved when public opinion demanded that he should take his proper place in the state, and exert the influence to which he was entitled as first prince of the blood. Had King Henry been a man of ability, who could rule his ministers instead of being ruled by them, there seems no reason to think that Duke Richard would have stirred. All through his life he was a man of cautious and moderate measures: but he would have been more than human if he had refrained from using his strength when he was shouldered aside and ignored by the faction led by the Beauforts, Suffolk, and Queen Margaret.

The loss of Normandy was followed by the first popular outbreak in England which had been seen for more than a generation. It was directed against the king's ministers and advisers, and appeared all over the southern shires. Already, before Formigny had been fought, a mob of mutinous soldiers had stoned to death Bishop Moleyns, the keeper of the Privy Seal, at Portsmouth (Jan., 1450). Two months later such a bitter outcry in Parliament was raised against Suffolk that, after he had been impeached, the timid king ordered him to leave the realm for the present. He took ship for Flanders, but was waylaid on the high seas by some vessels from London, and was murdered by the sailors. Who was at the bottom of this act of piracy was never discovered. (May 2, 1450.)

Suffolk murdered.

If the Queen and Somerset hoped that the unpopularity of the ministry might end with Suffolk's fall they were soon undeceived. The populace was still unsatisfied. In the month of June troubles broke out in many places:

Ayscough, Bishop of Salisbury, the king's confessor, was slain by rioters in his own diocese. There were risings in Sussex and Norfolk also, but the main focus of the trouble lay in Kent. It was fomented by a certain John Aylmer or Cade, a soldier of fortune who had served under York both in France and Ireland. He assumed the name of Mortimer, stated that he was a distant relative of Duke Richard, and pretended that he was acting in his interests. With a great mob of Kentishmen at his back he entered London (July 3, 1450), after beating the hasty levies which the ministers sent out against him. The Londoners joined him, and for a few days he was master of the streets: he used his power to execute Lord Say, the treasurer, and Crowmere, Sheriff of Kent, the chief officials who fell into his power. But Cade soon proved unable to keep his followers in hand: they fell to plundering, and so frightened the citizens that many of them took arms and aided the garrison of the Tower in driving the insurgents out of the city. On being promised a pardon the Kentishmen dispersed, but their leader, refusing to disarm, was hunted down and slain.

Cade's Rising.

Meanwhile Richard of York, hearing of the tumults in England, had left his post at Dublin and crossed St. George's Channel. When he came to land many of his followers flocked to join him, and it seemed likely that a new civil war might break out. But the duke contented himself with issuing manifestoes against the ministry, and setting on his partisans in Parliament to attack them. The Yorkist majority in the House of Commons tendered to the king a petition begging him to dismiss Somerset and his friends, but Henry was entirely in the hands of the Beauforts, and refused to listen to it. When Thomas Young, member for Bristol, spoke of the duke as rightful heir to the crown, he was sent to the Tower.

York still held back from violent measures, but if anything was yet wanting to complete Somerset's discredit with the nation it was the result of the next year's campaign in France. In 1451 the French threw themselves upon Aquitaine, which the government had wholly neglected during the domestic troubles. The Gascons did their best, but one after another all their cities fell before the French artillery. Bordeaux yielded in June and Bayonne in October, without having received any succour from England. Only Calais now remained unconquered of all the broad domain which Henry VI. had inherited on the Continent.

The loss of Aquitaine at last drove York to desperation. Raising his own retainers and those of the Nevilles and Mowbrays he marched on London. The king, at the head of a larger force, faced him at Dartford, in Kent, and there at a conference Henry promised to dismiss his present advisers and change his methods of governance. But when York had disbanded his army Somerset appeared again at the king's right hand, and Duke Richard found that he had been tricked (March, 1452). He was arrested, and only released after pledging himself never again to take arms. This promise he kept, under circumstances of great provocation, for three years (1452–5).

Meanwhile the last campaign of the Hundred Years' War was about to begin. The Gascons, sincerely attached to the English connection and oppressed by their new French governors, burst out into insurrection in the summer of 1452. To aid them Lord Talbot, now Earl of Shrewsbury, came over from England at the head of four or five thousand men. Aided by the insurgents he recovered Bordeaux and all the lands around it, and **Battle of Castillon.** during the winter of 1452–3 held his own with ease. But when summer came round the whole national levy of France marched into Aquitaine and laid siege to Castillon. Hurrying up to rescue it, the brave old earl resolved to storm the French lines of circumvallation. Forming his men in a deep column, contrary to the English custom, he launched them at the entrenchments. But the hostile artillery blew the head of the mass to pieces, Talbot himself was slain, and after a hard struggle the English and Gascons were cut to pieces (July 17, 1453). This battle settled the fate of

Aquitaine, for Somerset could not or would not send out further succours, and Bordeaux capitulated in October, after holding out gallantly for ten weeks.

A few days after the battle of Castillon, and long before it could be known in England, King Henry fell for the first time into a fit of madness, the result (it is said) of a sudden fright. For eighteen months he remained in a state of melancholy apathy, or rather idiocy, and was unable to discharge the simplest functions of royalty. This was in many ways the best thing for England that could have happened, and many years of trouble would have been avoided if he had never recovered. After a space Parliament met and appointed Duke Richard Protector of the realm, while Somerset was sent to the Tower. But some three months after her husband had gone mad, the Queen, after nine years of childless wedlock, gave birth to a son, a circumstance which changed the aspect of politics by cutting York out of the line of succession to the throne. He behaved, however, with correctness and moderation, acknowledged the infant prince as heir to the crown, and did homage to him. He acted as regent for more than a year, and did his best to bring the internal affairs of the kingdom into order: for the French war nothing could be done: with the second fall of Bordeaux all hope of retaining a foothold in Aquitaine had vanished.

The king's madness.

About mid-winter 1454-5 King Henry suddenly recovered his senses. The moment that he was convalescent his wife induced him to release Somerset from prison, and a few weeks later York and his friends were dismissed from all their offices, which were given back to the Beauforts and their partisans. A parliament was then summoned to meet at Leicester, which was to reverse all the acts of the Protectorate. Now at last Duke Richard lost his temper, and took arms at the head of his faction, after issuing a manifesto which denounced Somerset, not only as a minister of tried incapacity, but as a perjured traitor. The king, with a considerable armed following, was moving from London towards the Midlands, when the duke and his partisans fell upon him at St. Albans: there was a short but sharp fray in the streets, which ended in the victory of the Yorkists, due mainly to the hard fighting of the younger Richard Neville, the Earl of Warwick, who first broke through the Lancastrian barricades. Somerset was slain, and with him several peers of his faction: the king fell into the hands of the victors (May 22, 1455).

<small>First battle of St. Albans.</small>

This insignificant skirmish, in which neither side had more than 2000 men present, cost the lives of only a few scores of fighting men. But it was to be the prelude of a war of the most desperate and bloody kind, which was to mow down half the baronage of England. It came to be known as the "War of the Roses" from the white rose, which was the badge of the house of York, and the red rose, which was afterwards assumed as the token of the house of Lancaster.

At first it seemed possible that the battle of St. Albans might lead to a mere change of ministry, much desired by the majority of the nation. Duke Richard treated the captive king with all respect, and merely reinstated himself and his friends in power. The excitement of the battle had thrown Henry back into his melancholy madness, in which he lay for some months incapable of all action. The duke's term of power, however, lasted little more than a year: in October, 1456, the king, having recovered his senses once more, fell under the influence of his wife, who now put herself openly forward as head of the Loyalist faction in place of Somerset. By her advice the Yorkists were removed from office.

Three years of unrest and bickering followed (1456–59) before matters again came to a head. Each party meanwhile was preparing for the inevitable strife: the blood shed at St. Albans had made reconciliation impossible, and it was felt that the next struggle must lead to the extermination of one party or the other. Duke Richard saw that it would not avail him to attain once more to office, if he was always liable to be dismissed from it at the queen's pleasure: when forced to take arms again he must make his position secure. Margaret, on the other hand, was conscious that if she failed in the on-coming struggle the succession of her little son to his father's throne would be more than problematical. She was resolved to fight to the death for his rights, and spent all her time and energy in binding into a compact Lancastrian party those of the baronage who were not allied by blood or ancient friendship with the houses of York, Neville, and Mowbray. Beside the Beaufort clan, now headed by Henry, son of the Somerset who had fallen at St. Albans, she could count on the support of the Percies (old rivals of the Nevilles) in the North, of the Courtenays Earls of Devon in the West, of the Dukes of Buckingham and Exeter, and the Earls of Oxford and Shrewsbury, and of a body of barons decidedly more numerous than those who followed Duke Richard, though not individually so powerful.

All through 1458 both Yorkists and Lancastrians had been secretly arming for a new trial of strength. In the summer of 1459 the queen began to issue writs in her husband's name, bidding her partisans be ready to turn out in arms at a moment's notice. It was this fact, followed by a peremptory summons to the Yorkist leaders to present themselves before the king in person, which seems to have provoked the final outburst. In September Duke Richard raised his standard in the Mortimer lands on the Welsh border, while Salisbury called out the Neville tenants in the North Riding, and the young Earl of Warwick hurried over from Calais to join his father. The two Nevilles made their way to the west to join their kinsman, Warwick without difficulty, but Salisbury only after a sharp fight with the Loyalists of Cheshire and Staffordshire, on whom he inflicted a bloody check at Bloreheath. But the numerous supporters of York in London and the eastern counties had no time to join their chief before the fate of the campaign was settled. The king, showing for once in his life both energy and decision, had placed himself at the head of the levies of central England, and marched on Ludlow, where the insurgents lay. Their armies faced each other at Ludford across the flooded Teme, and a battle on a large scale seemed imminent: but the duke's partisans saw that they were much outnumbered, and many of them felt scruples at resisting their sovereign when he personally led his army to attack them: this time it was no question of opposing a Suffolk or a Somerset; the king himself, and not merely the king's name, was arrayed against them. When Henry and his host passed the Teme and advanced on the Yorkist camp, the insurgents melted away before his face without fighting, and the Lancastrians were victorious without striking a blow. Duke Richard escaped to Ireland, where he found a warm welcome: the two Neville earls escaped in a fishing-smack to Calais, where the garrison was devoted to Warwick, who had long been their governor (October, 1459).

The Rout of Ludford.

The "Rout of Ludford" placed the queen in a triumphant position: the Yorkists had put themselves in the wrong by their armed rebellion, and it would have been easy to crush them in their two last strongholds. But Margaret showed herself an incompetent ruler: instead of making a vigorous attempt to end the war, she set to work to proscribe and punish her enemies before they were completely disposed of. The duke and his chief followers were attainted, their lands were confiscated, some of their minor adherents were executed, but no assault in strength was made on Calais or on Ireland. The Yorkist party had time to recover from its panic, and the nation was shocked by the queen's violent actions— the most unwise of them was that she had allowed the open town of Newbury to be sacked merely because it belonged to the duke.

In June 1460, Warwick, who showed himself throughout the leading spirit in the Yorkist ranks, landed at Sandwich with a few hundred followers from Calais. The Kentishmen at once rose in arms to aid him: the Londoners opened their gates to him, though a Royalist garrison maintained itself in the

Battle of Northampton.

Tower; and Archbishop Bourchier, a cousin of York, brought the levies of the eastern counties to his aid. The Queen, taken by surprise, had called together her partisans from the Midland shires at Northampton, where they palisaded a strong entrenched camp. But Warwick hurried forward from London, stormed the fortifications, and routed the Lancastrians. King Henry was taken prisoner, while the captains of his host, the Duke of Buckingham and the Earl of Shrewsbury, were slain (July 10, 1460). The Queen and her young son escaped to the North, where they took refuge with the Earl of Northumberland.

Duke Richard arrived from Ireland too late to take part in his nephew's victory, and found the greater part of the realm at his feet. He called together a parliament, in which hot disputes broke out among his partisans as to the way in which the governance of the realm should be arranged. Twice already the plan of retaining King Henry on the throne and making York Protector had been tried and had failed. Many of the duke's advisers were of opinion that he might now set aside Henry, and declare himself king: there was no doubt that from the point of view of strict hereditary right the heir of the house of March and Clarence had a better title than the heir of Lancaster. Richard himself leaned to this alternative, but Warwick and the Nevilles were for a less violent change. They thought that Richard should be proclaimed Protector for life, and heir to the throne, while Henry should be allowed to reign in name so long as he lived. Personally the pious king was not unpopular, and no one wished him ill, but it was necessary to disinherit his young son Edward, in order that Queen Margaret might never again interfere in politics. This alternative was ultimately adopted: it bears a strong resemblance to the scheme formulated at the Treaty of Troyes in respect to the crown of France.

York, being named Protector for life, had now to subdue the parts of the realm where his title was not acknowledged. He sent against Wales, where the two

Tudors, Jasper and Owen,[1] step-brother and step father of King Henry, were in arms, his eldest son Edward Earl of March, a young man of eighteen, who had seen his first service in the field at Northampton. He himself, and his brother-in-law, Richard Neville Earl of Salisbury, marched into the North. There the Lancastrian interest was very strong: indeed, the Yorkists had little influence north of the Humber save in the Neville estates in the North Riding. The Queen, the young Duke of Somerset, and the Percies had raised a considerable army and were bent on fighting. York, undervaluing their numbers and overestimating the extent to which they had been demoralized by the defeat of Northampton, rashly engaged with them at Wakefield, though his forces amounted to only a third of theirs. He was surrounded and cut to pieces with the whole of his army: the Earl of Salisbury and Edmund of York, Richard's second son, a lad of sixteeen, were captured and put to death in cold blood by the victors. Their heads, with that of the duke himself, were struck off and placed on spikes over the gate of York (Dec. 30, 1460).

Battle of Wakefield.

This murder of prisoners and mutilation of the dead was by far the worst outrage which had yet happened in the struggle. It embittered the civil war into a blood-feud, and made the heirs of York and Salisbury pitiless for the future. Hitherto they had given quarter, but now they had the death and dishonour of their fathers to avenge. A change for the worse is at once visible in their action.

After the victory of Wakefield the Lancastrians flocked in from all sides to join the Queen, and she was able to march on London at the head of a formidable host. The task of opposing her fell on Warwick, who, by the deaths of his father and uncle, had become the undisputed head of his party, Edward of March being as yet young and little known. Warwick arrayed the Yorkists

[1] Some years after the death of Henry V. his widow, Catharine of France, had wedded Owen Tudor, a plain Welsh gentleman. Her two sons by him, Edmund and Jasper, were made Earls of Richmond and Pembroke by their half-brother the king. The former, who died young, was the father of Henry VII.

of London, Kent, and the eastern counties at St. Albans, and there awaited the hostile attack. It was delivered with great vigour on Feb. 17, 1461, and once more the Queen was victorious. Treachery or chance left a gap in the earl's line, through which the Lancastrians penetrated, and the routed host was pushed westward in its flight, leaving the road to London open. The king was recaptured by his friends, and his wife celebrated his deliverance by executing the two chief Yorkist prisoners who fell into her hands.

Second battle of St. Albans.

The fall of London now seemed so sure that the victorious Lancastrians spent eight days in settling the terms of capitulation at their leisure. This delay proved their ruin, and saved the capital. Edward of March had now beaten the Welsh levies of the Tudors at the battle of Mortimer's Cross (Feb. 2, 1461), and was already on the march for London when the news of the disaster at St. Albans reached him. At Chipping Norton Warwick joined him with the wrecks of his beaten host, and after a short conference they agreed to move on the capital and throw themselves into it, if it was not already in the enemy's power. By a forced march they reached it on the very day when it was to have been surrendered to the Queen (Feb. 26). The sudden arrival of 12,000 Yorkists within the walls changed the aspect of affairs: and the Londoners resolved to hold out. Margaret and her generals were not prepared for a siege: their army was discontented at being denied the sack of London, and was already beginning to melt home with the plunder which it had gathered in the Home counties. After some hesitation the Lancastrians determined to retire northward to gather reinforcements, and to throw the dangers of the offensive on their enemies. As they moved backward along the road to York they ravaged the country around in the most shameful manner.

It was this misbehaviour of the northern moss-troopers which mainly accounts for the sudden vehemence with which the Midlands now took up the cause of York:

hitherto they had been but lukewarm, but smarting under their losses they turned out in great force to join Edward of March and Richard of Warwick. The former, before starting on the campaign, was saluted by his followers as king, under the name of Edward IV. He claimed the crown as heir of Lionel of Clarence, ignoring the Lancastrian usurpation, and dated his reign from March 1461, though his title did not receive Parliamentary sanction till November. Thus with him triumphed the cause of hereditary right, as opposed to that theory of election by the nation represented in Parliament, under which the Lancastrian house had held the throne.

Edward IV. made King.

Allowing only a few days of rest to their army, Warwick and King Edward followed the Lancastrians towards York, gathering up on their way numerous levies from the Eastern and Midland shires. On March 28th the enemy was found lying behind the river Aire. After driving in his rearguard by a skirmish at Ferrybridge, the Yorkists crossed the stream and came upon the Queen's host drawn up on the hillside of Towton. Next day (Palm Sunday, March 29, 1461) the bloodiest battle of the Wars of the Roses was fought. Both sides were in great force, and contemporary writers thought that as many as 60,000 Lancastrians and 45,000 Yorkists were engaged,—figures that cannot be trusted for a moment. In a blinding snow-storm the Yorkists climbed the hillside and ranged themselves opposite their foes: after a preliminary discharge of arrows the hosts clashed together all along the line, and remained locked together for many hours of close fighting with sword and axe. Towards evening a flank attack made by the Duke of Norfolk settled the result of the battle, and the Queen's army turned to fly. Besides those who fell in the pursuit great numbers were drowned in the flooded stream of the Cock, which lay just behind their position. The slaughter was very great, especially among the barons and knights, who could not easily fly in their heavy mail. The Earl of Northumberland and four other peers were slain: the

Battle of Towton.

Earls of Devon and Wiltshire, and a great number of knights and squires captured in the pursuit, were beheaded, in revenge for the slaying of Salisbury and Prince Edmund after Wakefield.

The Queen, with her husband and her young son, fled from York into Scotland the moment that the result of the battle was known. With them went the young Duke of Somerset, almost the only Lancastrian of note who escaped from the field alive. The party was crushed beyond hope of recovery, and though its desperate partisans held out for nearly three years more in Wales and on the Scottish border, they were never able to shake the power of the new king. Indeed, England south of the Tees was free from civil war from the day of Towton onwards.

The lingering struggle in Northumberland was only sustained by two supports, the Queen's untiring energy, and the desperate hatred for the Nevilles which filled the hearts of the Percies and the other nobles of the north. Margaret bought aid from Scotland by ceding Berwick to King James III.: she crossed to France and wrung money and auxiliaries from the stingy Louis XI. by promising to give over Calais to him. But all her efforts came to nought: the great Northumbrian fortresses of Alnwick and Bamborough were taken by the Earl of Warwick (1462). By the aid of her French troops she recovered them for a moment, but this success was only to lead to a second disaster: Warwick returned and blew the great northern strongholds to pieces with his artillery (1463). The Scots grew tired of the war: King Louis would give no more aid when he found that Calais was not likely to come into his hands. The final desperate rally of the northern Lancastrians was crushed at the fights of Hedgeley Moor (April 15) and Hexham (May 13th, 1464). After this last victory the few surviving chiefs of the loyalists fell into Warwick's hands, and when he had beheaded the Duke of Somerset and the Lords Roos and Hungerford, the long resistance collapsed for lack of leaders. At last there was no man

The struggle in the North.

left in England who did not bow his head before King Edward and his great vicegerent, Richard Neville. King Henry himself, wandering hopelessly in disguise through the realm that had once been his own, was captured and consigned to the Tower, where he lingered for six years in pious melancholy.

<small>Henry VI. a prisoner.</small>

CHAPTER XIII.

RICHARD THE KING-MAKER AND EDWARD THE KING.
1464-1483.

While the struggle with the last survivors of the Lancastrian faction was still in progress, the governance of England had been in the hands of the Neville clan. Richard of Warwick, "the King-maker", the head of the house, and by far its most able representative, had been continually in the field as the leader of King Edward's armies; George Neville, Archbishop of York (Warwick's brother), was chancellor; John Neville Lord Montague (another brother) was regarded as the king's confidential councillor; he had also commanded at Hexham and Hedgeley Moor. William Neville Lord Falconberg had been made Earl of Kent for his services at Towton, and several other members of the family were high in place about the king. The house and its connections had formed the backbone of the Yorkist party, and its members thought themselves entitled to good payment for their services. If Edward IV. had been a weak ruler the domination of the Nevilles might have continued all through his reign. But the young king was far from being a nonentity: he was able, obstinate, selfish, and ungrateful, the last of men to suffer himself to be made the tool of his mother's relations. As long as the Lancastrians still made head against him he was content to use the services of Warwick and his brothers, but now that his throne was safe he intended to rule after his own

RISE OF THE WOODVILLES. 141

will and inclination. He was quite competent to do so: at Mortimer's Cross and Towton he had already shown that he was a good soldier; he had a clear head, a hard heart, and no scruples. His weak point was a love of pleasure and debauchery, which sometimes led him to waste his time in idleness; but when prompt and decisive action was required he always shed his sloth, and set to work with an energy and ability which startled his enemies.

The first rift between the king and the Nevilles appeared in the year 1464, just after the last hopes of the Lancastrians had been crushed at Hexham. The king was now twenty-three, and it was high time for him to wed: with his apparent consent Warwick commenced a negotiation for his marriage with the sister of the Queen of France. The Neville foreign policy had always been to ally England to France, and to distrust the King of France's rival, Charles the Rash, the great Duke of Burgundy. Suddenly Edward announced that the French match must be dropped, because he was married already. He had become infatuated with a beautiful widow seven years older than himself. *King Edward's marriage.* Elizabeth Woodville was the daughter of Lord Rivers, a Lancastrian peer, and her first husband, Sir John Grey, another prominent Lancastrian, had fallen at St. Albans. Caring nothing for the disparity of rank nor for the disloyal traditions of Elizabeth's family, Edward had secretly married her, and kept the matter dark for six months (May–October, 1464). When he vouchsafed to declare what he had done, Warwick had at once to abandon his negotiations with Louis XI., and was much displeased at the manner in which he had been tricked.

The king soon began to display an exaggerated fondness for his wife's numerous relations, to place them about his person, and to seek wealthy marriages for them. We cannot doubt that his conduct was dictated by policy, and not by a real regard for the Woodvilles and Greys, who were a greedy and grasping crew. He wished to surround himself with persons entirely dependent on his favour, as a check on the haughty and self-reliant Neville clan. For the same reason, he created a number of new peers to counterbalance the Neville family group in the House of Lords. For two years there was no open breach between Edward and Warwick, but in June, 1467, the king dismissed George Neville, the chancellor, openly disavowed Warwick and his policy, and put himself entirely in the hands of his new friends. His change of views was completed by the formation of an alliance with the Duke of Burgundy, to whom he gave his sister Margaret in marriage.

Edward quarrels with the Nevilles.

To break so rudely and openly with the Nevilles was unwise: the family was powerful in nearly every part of England, and Warwick had been for so long the figurehead of the Yorkist party that most of its older members looked to him and not to the king for guidance. Moreover, the Woodvilles were making themselves hated for their pride and shameless greed. A typical instance of their conduct was the marriage of young John Woodville, the queen's brother, to the Dowager Duchess of Norfolk, who was old enough to have been his grandmother, but possessed wealth enough to tempt him into the match. Noting the unpopularity which was gathering around Edward, Warwick began to make quiet preparations for resuming his old position, even though he might have to use force in the process. He enlisted in his cause the king's brother, George Duke of Clarence, an ambitious and discontented young man, by giving him the hand of his eldest daughter, Isabel Neville, on whom (since the great earl had no male issue) the larger half of his vast estates would some day devolve.

In July, 1469, thinking matters ripe for his interference, Warwick set his followers to work. His nephew Sir Henry Fitzhugh and his cousin Sir Henry Neville took arms in Yorkshire, with a programme much like that which the Lords Appellant had used against Richard II., or the early Yorkists against Suffolk and Somerset. The king must be freed from unworthy favourites, and provided with a respectable and responsible ministry, *i.e.* replaced in his former dependence on the house of

Neville. This rising is often called the rebellion of "Robin of Redesdale", an assumed name adopted by one of its leaders, Sir John Conyers. War- wick had passed the word around among his friends and adherents to support the rising, but did not appear himself. Soon the rebel army swelled to formidable proportions, moved south and routed the troops which the king sent against it, under the Earls of Pembroke and Devon,[1] at Edgecot Field, near Banbury. Edward after the battle saw his army disperse, and fell into the hands of the rebels. Warwick and Clarence then appeared upon the scene, and assumed the custody of the king's person. Edward was treated with formal courtesy, but placed for a time in safe keeping at Middleham Castle, a Neville stronghold in Yorkshire. His favourites fared much worse: the queen's father Rivers, her brother John Woodville, and the Earls of Devon and Pembroke, were all beheaded by the rebels, with Warwick's full approval. Greedy upstarts as they were, they did not deserve to die without a trial, and their bloody end shocked the whole Yorkist party.

Robin of Redesdale's rebellion.

After keeping the king two months under restraint (Aug.–Sept., 1469), Warwick released him, thinking that he had been taught the necessary lesson, and would for the future refrain from offending the Neville clan. As a matter of fact, Edward's spirit was not broken, and his only thought was to revenge himself on the earl and Clarence. Six months later he got his opportunity: a Lancastrian insurrection broke out in Lincolnshire in March, 1470, and to suppress it the king gathered a large army, whose leaders were carefully chosen from among the enemies of the Nevilles. After dispersing the rebels near Stamford, in a fight often called "Lose-Coat field",[2] the king suddenly wheeled about, and marched against Warwick and Clarence, who

The Lincolnshire rising.

---

[1] These men are not, of course, the Lancastrian Earls, Jasper Tudor and John Courtenay, but Yorkists (named Herbert and Stafford) to whom the titles of the others had been given.

[2] Lose-Coat field was so called from the haste in which the rebels cast off their cassocks, in order to fly the quicker.

were coming from Coventry to join him with a small force. He was resolved to treat them just as they had treated him in the preceding year:[1] having caught them unprepared he hunted them across England, and finally forced them to embark at Dartmouth, and flee to France (March, 1470).

The great earl had fallen so easily because he had not been granted time to call together his numerous adherents: if the king had lingered, Warwick's expulsion would have cost him much heavy fighting. He was now master of his realm again, but not for long. His enemy was bent on revenge, and had made up his mind to forget all his old grudges against Margaret of Anjou and the Lancastrians. At the court of Louis XI. the earl met the exiled queen, and made his peace with her. They agreed to join their forces in order to crush Edward IV., and Warwick undertook to replace Henry VI. on the throne: as a pledge of reconciliation, his younger daughter, Anne Neville, was betrothed to Prince Edward, the heir of the Lancastrian house. Warwick soon set to work to use all his powers of intrigue: his emissaries overran the whole of England, bidding his partisans to be prepared for a rising in the autumn; while Queen Margaret sent similar warnings to the survivors of her party.

Warwick in exile.

In September the plot had been prepared: Lord Fitzhugh, a brother-in-law of Warwick, got up an unimportant rising in the North to attract the king's attention. Edward took the bait, and when he had reached York the earl slipped across the Channel and raised his banner in Devonshire, a district where the Lancastrian party was strong. When the signal was given the retainers of the Nevilles rose in arms in every shire, and the king had to turn southward: he had only reached Nottingham when he found that Warwick's brother Montague had led over to the enemy the whole of the levies of the Midlands which

[1] Some think that Warwick was really implicated in the Lincolnshire rising, and the king stated so at the time, but it seems more likely that he was not. If he had been organizing the business he would not have been caught unprepared, and the leaders of the rebellion were all old Lancastrians.

had been gathered together to resist the invasion. The king's own soldiery began to melt away from him, and in despair he rode hard for the coast and took ship at Lynn with his young brother Richard Duke of Gloucester, Lord Hastings, and a few scores of faithful followers. He reached the Netherlands in safety and was kindly received by Charles the Rash, his brother-in-law. The Duke of Burgundy was anxious to oblige any enemy of his old foe Louis XI. of France.

Warwick drives out Edward IV.

The power of the Nevilles had been vindicated, and Warwick might indeed call himself the "King-maker" when he drew Henry VI. from his prison in the Tower and replaced him on his long-lost throne. Edward had been beaten without a blow struck, and his wife and young daughters were at the earl's mercy as hostages. He did not, however, disturb them when they took sanctuary at Westminster. The position of the conqueror was a difficult one: he was distrusted by the Lancastrians, and himself distrusted them: Clarence, his chief supporter, was discontented at the restoration of the old king: he had hoped that his father-in-law would have given him the crown instead of replacing it on the head of Henry. Edward was known to have many partisans, but how many no one could say, since they had been given no opportunity of displaying themselves. Meanwhile a ministry, partly composed of Warwick's friends, partly of Lancastrians, was put in power; and for the moment all was quiet. Queen Margaret and her son very unwisely lingered in France: they should have crossed the Channel when their party had triumphed.

In March, 1471, came the last development of the long strife between the King-maker and his former master. Edward IV. was furnished with 50,000 florins and 1200 mercenaries by the Duke of Burgundy, and sailed forth from Holland to try his fortune once more. He landed in Yorkshire, giving out at first that he was only come to claim his father's duchy, and did not ask for the crown or intend civil war. By the inexcusable carelessness of Montague, who was commanding in the North, he was allowed to slip across the Trent and to reach Leicester, where a considerable body of his partisans joined him. It seemed probable, however, that he would soon be crushed by numbers, for hostile forces began to close around him on all sides, and Warwick himself advanced to Coventry, which had been appointed as the mustering place of his host. From this rather desperate position Edward was rescued by the treachery of his brother George of Clarence. The duke had been commissioned to raise the western Midlands in King Henry's name: but when he approached Coventry he swerved aside and joined the invaders with seven or eight thousand men. This made Edward so strong that Warwick could not fight him till he had received reinforcements. While the earl was waiting, his adversary made a desperate dash for London, and was admitted within its walls by a sudden rising of his partisans (April 11, 1471). But Warwick was now close at his heels with all his host, and till he was beaten off nothing had really been secured. Accordingly the Yorkists marched out and met their pursuers at Barnet, where on April 14 a desperate battle took place. It was fought in a dense fog, a circumstance which proved fatal to the great earl, for two corps of his army mistook each other for enemies and came to blows. When they recognized each other, each thought the other had deserted to the king, and both cried "treachery" and fled. The remainder of the Kingmaker's men stood their ground but were overwhelmed by numbers and cut to pieces. Warwick himself and his brother Montague were both left dead upon the field.

The return of King Edward.

Battle of Barnet.

On the very day of Barnet, Queen Margaret and her son landed at Weymouth and put themselves at the head of an army which the Beauforts had gathered in Somerset and Devon. Hearing of Warwick's defeat and death they resolved to make their way towards Wales, a great Lancastrian stronghold. But by a forced march King Edward threw himself across their path and forced them to fight at Tewkesbury with the unfordable Severn at their backs. After a hard struggle the Lan-

Battle of Tewkesbury.

castrians were beaten from their position, and all who could not fly fast were slain, captured, or driven into the river. The young Prince Edward was killed as he cried in vain for quarter and called on the name of "his brother Clarence": with him fell the Earl of Devon and Lord Wenlock. Edmund, the last Duke of Somerset of the Beaufort line, was captured and executed with ten other prisoners of rank (May 4, 1471). Queen Margaret also fell into the victor's hands: her life was spared, but with a perfectly gratuitous cruelty Edward ordered her harmless husband to be secretly put to death in the Tower. Now that his only son was dead Henry was no longer valuable as a hostage, and was made away with. His murderer gave out that he died "of pure displeasure and melancholy". *Murder of Henry VI.*

So ended in one common disaster the dynasty of Lancaster and the great house of Neville. The male line of John of Gaunt was extinct: the female line was only represented by the King of Portugal and the Queen of Castile, who descended from two of his daughters, and by the Lady Margaret Beaufort the last of the Somersets. She had a son by her first husband Edmund Tudor, Earl of Richmond, and this young boy was one day to reign under the name of Henry VII. The vast estates of Warwick were divided between his two daughters, the Duchess of Clarence and the Princess Anne the widow of Prince Edward. The latter was forced to marry the king's youngest brother, Richard Duke of Gloucester, so that all the broad Neville, Montacute, and Beauchamp lands passed into the hands of the royal family.

Edward had yet twelve years to reign: they contrast strongly with the troublous times between 1460 and 1471, for their annals are lacking in interest and incident. The king was strong-handed enough to rule as he pleased, and might have become a tyrant had he been more restless and energetic. But habits of sloth grew upon him, and he wasted much of his time on pleasures, lawful and unlawful, and on riotous living. Before he was forty he had ruined his constitution and had grown grossly corpulent and unwieldy. His rule was far more autocratic than that of the Lancastrian house: between 1478 and 1483 he did not call Parliament together, and he often indulged in the unconstitutional practice of raising "benevolences" or forced loans not sanctioned by parliamentary authority. But he can hardly be called an oppressive ruler: his arbitrary acts did not affect the bulk of his subjects, and his financial exactions were moderate, for he was much wealthier than his predecessors owing to the vast amounts of confiscated land, belonging to the followers of Lancaster and Warwick, which had fallen into his hands. After 1475 he had another source of revenue.

Treaty of Pecquigny. In alliance with Charles of Burgundy he invaded France, and advanced as far as Peronne in Picardy. But the wily Louis XI. offered to buy him off, by paying down a great sum of money and guaranteeing him an annual pension as long as peace should endure. Edward threw over his ally and greedily closed with the offer. By the Treaty of Pecquigny (13th Aug., 1475) he received 75,000 gold crowns in ready money, 50,000 more as a ransom for the unfortunate Margaret of Anjou, and the guarantees for the payment of 50,000 crowns per annum as long as he should live. He at once retired from France, and for the rest of his life was paid the subsidy with great regularity.

The main anxiety of Edward during these years arose from the discontent of his brother George of Clarence. The treachery of the duke in the years 1469–70 could never be forgotten, and the king always viewed him with suspicion. Clarence did his best to justify these doubts: his behaviour was captious, insolent, and overbearing. In 1477 he provoked Edward to great wrath by putting to death on his own authority and without a proper trial a lady named Ankaret Twyndow, whom he accused of having caused by sorcery the death of his wife the Duchess Isabel. On another occasion he tried to marry Margaret, the heiress of Burgundy, without Edward's leave. In 1478 the brothers had a violent quarrel about the arrest and execution of some of Clarence's followers for treason.

It ended in the duke's being sent to the Tower: soon after Edward called together a Parliament and accused his brother in person before the Peers. **Clarence executed.** Clarence was, he said, incorrigible, and "he would not be answerable for the weal, public peace, and tranquillity of the realm if such loathly offences should be pardoned". The Lords could do no less than find the accused guilty, when the king acted as prosecutor. A fortnight later "false, fleeting, perjured Clarence" was put to death in the Tower. A tradition dating back to the very year of his execution declares that he was drowned in a butt of Malmsey wine: but nothing is really known of the details of his end.

Edward survived his brother for five years: his health was steadily growing worse, but he made no attempt to break himself of his evil habits, and as he became less fit for business handed over much of the conduct of affairs to his youngest brother Richard Duke of Gloucester and his chamberlain Lord Hastings, the two faithful partisans who had never shrunk from his side in all the troubles of the evil days in 1469-71.

The last important event in the reign was a short war with Scotland in 1482, caused partly by the raids of the moss-troopers of the Border into Northumberland, partly by the intrigues of the exiled **War with Scotland.** Duke of Albany, who stirred up England against his brother James III. for his own private ends. Gloucester held the command, since the king was too ill to take the field, and distinguished himself by retaking Berwick, which had been held by the Scots since Margaret of Anjou made it over to them in 1461. He ravaged the Lowlands till the Scottish king sued for peace, but the negotiations were still unfinished when news came that King Edward was dead. Though only in his forty-second year his constitution was worn out, and he succumbed to an attack of ague of no special virulence (March 30, 1483). Thoroughly selfish, cruel, and debauched, he was one of the worst men who have sat on the English throne, but it cannot be said that he was an inefficient ruler.

The country was not unprosperous under his hand, in spite of all the wars and rumours of wars which had passed over it. The nobles and their retainers had been thinned by the sword and axe, but the storm had passed far above the heads of the majority of the nation. Taxation was light, trade and commerce were not unprosperous: England in short has seen much worse days under much better kings.

CHAPTER XIV.

RICHARD III. 1483-1485.

Edward IV. had been the father of a large family; but he had been cut off at so early an age that the two sons and five daughters whom he left behind him were all very young. Elizabeth, his eldest child, was only seventeen; Edward, Prince of Wales, his heir, was five years younger; Richard of York, his second son, but nine. It was obvious that several years of regency must elapse before the young king could take up the reins of government. Edward IV. had made no arrangements on his death-bed for nominating a regent, but there were only two possible persons who could be thought of for the post. One was the queen dowager, the other Richard of Gloucester, the first prince of the blood. It was at once seen that trouble would come of their rivalry: Elizabeth's success would mean danger to Gloucester, for her kindred, the Greys and Woodvilles, were old enemies of the duke. But the game seemed at first to be in her hands, for her son was at Ludlow under charge of his uncle, Anthony Woodville Earl Rivers, the chief of the clan. The queen's kindred held the young king's person, and "possession is nine points of the law". A less wily and resolute adversary than Richard of Gloucester would have yielded the game; but the duke was a man of a cunning and ambition unsuspected even by those who knew him best. He had hitherto been known only as a good soldier, a capable administrator, and a most faithful servant of the late king. Unlike his brother, George of Clarence, he was a prince of a sober and cautious demeanour, and made public pretensions to piety which his private life did not altogether bear out. No one dreamed that he would prove the most unscrupulous man of his unscrupulous house, and that he was prepared to wade to power through streams of innocent blood. Richard was often pictured by Tudor writers as a sort of deformed and unnatural monster: they said that he was dwarfish, hump-backed, and hideous. But though his left arm and shoulder were smaller than his right, and his stature rather small, his exterior was not unpleasing: none of the line of York were wanting in good looks, and Richard's worst drawback was the shifty and suspicious glance which all his portraits display. He had only reached the age of thirty-one when his brother died, but his ability had never been doubted since the day when as a lad of eighteen he commanded the Yorkist right wing at Barnet and Tewkesbury.

When the funeral of Edward IV. had taken place Lord Rivers proceeded to bring the young king up to London. There it was intended that his coronation should take place, and that the council should nominate a regent or a protector to carry on the business of the realm. When the royal cortége arrived at Stoney Stratford it was met by the Duke of Gloucester and his friend and supporter Henry Duke of Buckingham, the lineal representative of Thomas of Woodstock, and the younger line of Edward III.'s descendants.[1] Rivers must have noted with some alarm that the two dukes had brought with them armed retainers in numbers that were wholly unnecessary for the occasion. But he did not suspect how near was the blow that he dreaded: on the next day, as the cavalcade was starting again for London, Gloucester's retainers laid hands on Rivers and on Sir Richard Grey, the queen's second son, and threw them into bonds (April 30, 1483).

[1] See table on page 160.

They were hastily sent up to the duke's northern stronghold of Middleham, while the young king was taken on to the capital by his uncle. Queen Elizabeth saw that her cause was ruined, and took sanctuary at Westminster: her eldest son, the Marquis of Dorset, and her brother Edward Woodville fled to France.

Richard seizes the king.

Gloucester meanwhile, on arriving at London, dismissed the ministers, and appointed partisans of his own to their places. He then summoned Parliament to meet, proposing (as men thought) to have his nephew duly crowned and himself appointed protector. But soon an incident occurred which showed that his designs were not so simple as had been supposed. There were in the council many magnates who were glad to see the Woodvilles driven away, but wished for no further change. The chief of them was Lord Hastings, an old and faithful friend of Edward IV. Gloucester seems to have spent some days in sounding these men, to see how far they were ready to follow him. When he was clear upon the point he arranged a dramatic scene. The council had met in the Tower, and the duke seemed all smiles, when suddenly he withdrew for a moment, and then returning with a changed countenance began to declare that he had discovered a plot against his life. Sorcery was being practised against him, he said, and he asked what should be done to those implicated in the matter—the queen dowager, Jane Shore (the late king's favourite), and certain others, whom he would not name. Hastings, much surprised and somewhat alarmed, faltered that "*If* they had so done they were worthy of heinous punishment". "I tell thee they *have* done it, and that I will prove on thy body, traitor!" thundered the duke. He struck the table, armed men rushed in, and Hastings was dragged down to the courtyard and beheaded on a log. At the same time Lord Stanley, Rotheram Archbishop of York, and Morton Bishop of Ely, were taken into custody (June 13, 1483).

Murder of Hastings.

Having purged the council of the young king's true

RICHARD SEIZES THE CROWN.

friends, Gloucester was omnipotent. He now proceeded to further measures of ominous significance. Edward's younger brother, the little Duke of York, was taken out of his mother's hands, the queen being half cajoled half frightened into letting him quit the sanctuary and join his brother in the Tower. Thus Gloucester had both the heirs to the throne in his power. He then began to pack London with armed men drawn from his estates in the North, to whom were added those of his fellow-conspirator, Buckingham. It seems that no one save this young duke, and perhaps John Lord Howard, knew how far Gloucester's designs extended. Their aid had been bought by enormous gifts: the protector had granted to Buckingham the custody of all the royal castles in Wales and the West Country, and promised Howard the duchy of Norfolk, to which he had some claims in right of his mother.

The plea on which Richard had determined to strike at his nephews' right to the throne was that Edward IV.'s marriage with Elizabeth Woodville was invalid. He maintained that it had been celebrated in private, and without the proper ecclesiastical forms (which was partly true), and also that Edward had been previously betrothed to Lady Eleanor Talbot, a statement for which no real corroboration has ever been found. The princes, therefore, he said, were illegitimate children: Clarence had left a son and daughter, but his attainder in 1478 had "corrupted their blood", and they could make no claim through him. Richard himself, therefore, was "the very sure and true heir of the house of York". This preposterous theory was first set forth by the duke's chaplain, Dr. Shaw, in a sermon at St. Paul's on June 22. On the 24th, Buckingham made a harangue to the same effect to the mayor and aldermen of London at the Guildhall: overawed by the armed men about them the citizens made no objection. On the 25th a larger meeting was held, to which all the peers in London and many other men of note were bidden: a petition was laid before them to which they

Richard claims the crown.

were requested to give their consent; it implored Gloucester to assume the crown as the only true representative of the royal house. To their eternal disgrace the assembly bowed before the display of arms in the streets, and not a voice was raised to refuse the petition. Gloucester, after some hypocritical show of hesitation, assented to the request contained in it: next day he was proclaimed king, and on July 6th was crowned under the name of Richard III.

The moment that he was certain of success the new king had sent orders to the North for the execution of his enemies, Rivers and Grey: they were dead before he was crowned. But their faction was not extinguished: it had only been taken unprepared by the extreme swiftness with which Richard had acted. Before he had been a month on the throne a conspiracy was already on foot to overthrow him and restore Edward V. Its chiefs were Thomas Grey Marquis of Dorset, Lionel Woodville Bishop of Salisbury, and Thomas St. Leger, who had married the king's sister Anne. Richard got wind of the conspiracy, and thought to frustrate it with ease by the most abominable of expedients. He hastily sent word from Warwick, where he chanced to be at the moment, to order the secret murder of the young princes in the Tower. The wicked deed was done on or about the 9th of August, 1483: the boys were smothered, and their bodies hurriedly interred under a staircase, where they were found nearly two hundred years after, when some repairs were in progress in 1674. It was soon known that the princes were dead: the feeling throughout the country was one of horror: many atrocities had been committed during the Wars of the Roses, but not one that could vie with this. It may be said that Richard ruined himself by it: no man whose heart and mind retained any regard for righteousness could serve the tyrant faithfully for the future. Usurpation was one thing, the gratuitous murder of innocent children another. From this moment onward Richard felt that every man's hand was against him: not even those on

Murder of the princes.

REBELLION AND DEATH OF BUCKINGHAM. 155

whom he had heaped the most lavish gifts could be trusted.

The best proof of this was that the conspiracy, far from being crushed by the crime in the Tower, gathered force from it, and was joined by many who had hitherto held aloof. Chief of these was the Duke of Buckingham, who had hitherto acted as Richard's right-hand man. Though he had been given all that he asked, he cast in his lot with the rebels, not urging his own claim to the throne (which was not much worse than Richard's) but consenting to back that of another. For the conspirators, hearing of the death of Edward V., had resolved to rise in the names of the houses of York and Lancaster combined. Elizabeth, the eldest daughter of Edward IV., might marry Henry Tudor, son of Margaret, Countess of Richmond, and heir of the Beauforts. His Lancastrian claim was a poor one, but the only one that could be brought forward: no one thought of urging that of the distant Queen of Spain.[1]

In October, 1483, the insurrection broke out, Buckingham raising the Welsh border, while Dorset, St. Leger, and the Courtenays mustered their retainers in Devon, and other leaders unfurled their banners at Salisbury and Maidstone. The Earl of Richmond with some mercenaries hired in Brittany was to land at Plymouth and head the rising. For the last time in his life luck favoured Richard: an extraordinary and prolonged downpour of rain checked the communication of the rebels, and so swelled the Severn that Buckingham could not cross it to join his friends. Richmond was beaten back by storms and was unable to land. The king meanwhile, with such levies as he could raise, struck right and left at his foes. Buckingham's Welshmen dispersed, and he himself was captured and executed (Nov. 2). His failure awed the rebels in the south, who made no stand against Richard: St. Leger was caught and beheaded by his brother-in-law: the rest of the leaders escaped to France. Rich-

Buckingham's rebellion crushed.

[1] See tables on pages 160 and 161.

mond returned to Brittany without having set his foot ashore.

The failure of this first movement gave the king a short respite of eighteen months. They were a time of trouble, for everyone knew that the attempt would be repeated at the earliest opportunity. Richard lived in a state of miserable suspicion, knowing that there was treachery around him, but generally unable to strike for want of full knowledge. When he could lay hands on a foe he made away with him, even descending so far as to hang the unfortunate Collingbourn, a Wiltshire squire whose offence was that he had composed the rhyme—

> "The Cat, the Rat, and Lovel the Dog
> Rule all England under the Hog"—

in which Richard's ministers William Catesby, Sir Richard Ratcliffe, and Francis Lord Lovel, as well as the king's personal badge of the White Boar, were held up to scorn.

The Parliament met early in 1484 and a considerable parade of benevolent and constitutional legislation was made. But Richard's position was too uncertain to allow him to carry out any real reforms: having, for example, allowed "Benevolences" to be formally abolished, he was a few months later in such dire need of money that he had to have recourse to them again in spite of his handsome promises. Perpetual alarms of rebellion, and the need to retain his supporters in good temper by lavish gifts, conspired to keep his pocket always empty.

In April, 1484, the king's position was notably weakened by the death of his only child Edward, whom he had created Prince of Wales. Compelled to name an heir in his stead, Richard selected his nephew John de la Pole, Earl of Lincoln,[1] the son of his eldest sister. He could not fall back on Clarence's son, a more natural choice, as to do so would have falsified his own claim to the crown, which depended on Clarence's attainder. Not quite a year after Prince Edward's death his mother Queen Anne,

---

[1] It may be of interest to point out that this heir-apparent to the English throne was the great-grandson of the poet Chaucer.

the King-maker's daughter, followed him to the grave. Her end is said to have been hastened by her husband's ill-concealed intention of getting rid of her by divorce or otherwise, in order that he might marry a wife who would bring him another heir. When she was dead Richard is said for a moment to have thought of marrying his niece Elizabeth, the elder sister of the victims of the Tower. But the universal horror expressed by the nation, and brought to his notice by his own most trusty followers, caused him to abandon the horrid project.

When the summer of 1485 had come round, the exiles, who had never ceased to weave plans for a second invasion, tried their fortune once more. Henry Earl of Richmond had borrowed a little money from the French government, and with it had raised some 1200 continental mercenaries. He sailed from Harfleur on August 1: with him were the last survivors of the old Lancastrian party, his uncle Jasper Tudor Earl of Pembroke, and John de Vere Earl of Oxford, as well as the representatives of the Yorkist factions whom Richard III. had crushed, headed by Sir Edward Woodville. *Henry of Richmond invades England.* It seemed foolhardy to attack England with such a small force, but the invaders knew that their way had been prepared for them, and that aid would be forthcoming from many secret sympathizers. Landing at Milford Haven they were soon joined by some of the Welsh gentry, who gladly rallied round the red dragon of the Tudors. When they reached the Severn the retainers of the old Lancastrian house of the Talbots, Earls of Shrewsbury, came to their aid. But still when they faced King Richard at Bosworth Field in Leicestershire they could only put 5000 men in line against the 14,000 in the royal host. Nevertheless the Earl of Oxford marshalled his men in two small columns and led them up hill to attack the king. His confidence was justified: when the clash of battle came, half of Richard's army refused to close and hung back. The rest fought feebly, save where the king himself and his one trusty partisan, John Howard Duke of Norfolk, maintained their ground. Ere long a fatal blow was struck by two old Yorkists, Lord Stanley and his brother Sir William, who had pledged themselves to aid the invader. Coming on the field with fresh levies from Cheshire and Lancashire, they attacked the royalists in the flank. King Richard's army at once broke up, with shouts of "Treason!" Seeing himself betrayed the usurper refused to fly, and setting his face towards Richmond's banner cut his way as far as his adversary's person before he was borne down and hewn to pieces. With him fell the Duke of Norfolk, Lord Ferrers, and Sir Richard Ratcliffe, "the Rat" of poor Collingbourn's rhyme. Of the victorious army less than a hundred men fell, of the vanquished no very great number more—the whole matter had been settled by treason and not by hard fighting (Aug. 22, 1485). Richard had climbed to power by treachery, and by treachery he met with a righteous retribution. His body, stark naked and pierced by half a dozen wounds, was thrown across a horse and sent back for burial to Leicester, the place from which he had gone forth in royal state on the previous day.

Battle of Bosworth.

Thus ended the Wars of the Roses, one of the most sordid and depressing epochs in the history of England. They had begun in a justifiable attempt to displace a corrupt and incapable ministry: but soon they had become a mere blood-feud between the great baronial houses. A yet worse stage had been reached in the struggle between Warwick and Edward IV., when the personal dislike between a selfish and ungrateful king and an arrogant and unscrupulous subject kept the realm disturbed for year after year. They closed in the most disgraceful scene of all: peers and people had accepted a bloodthirsty and hypocritical usurper as king in a moment of unworthy panic, and only got rid of him by deliberate treachery on the battle-field.

England has suffered more misery in other periods—the Wars of the Roses passed lightly above the heads of citizens and peasants, and were only fatal to the quarrelsome baronage. But she has seldom or never been in a

NATIONAL DEMORALIZATION.   159

worse moral state than in the years 1455–85. The constant and violent changes of rulers, the unending chain of attainders and executions, the easy swearing of allegiance to one king and another, the enormous part played by treachery and bad faith in politics, had swept away all the old traditions of constitutional order and good governance. To restore the realm to a healthy state there was needed the hard discipline of a century of rule by the strong-handed house of Tudor.

160 ENGLAND AND THE HUNDRED YEARS' WAR.

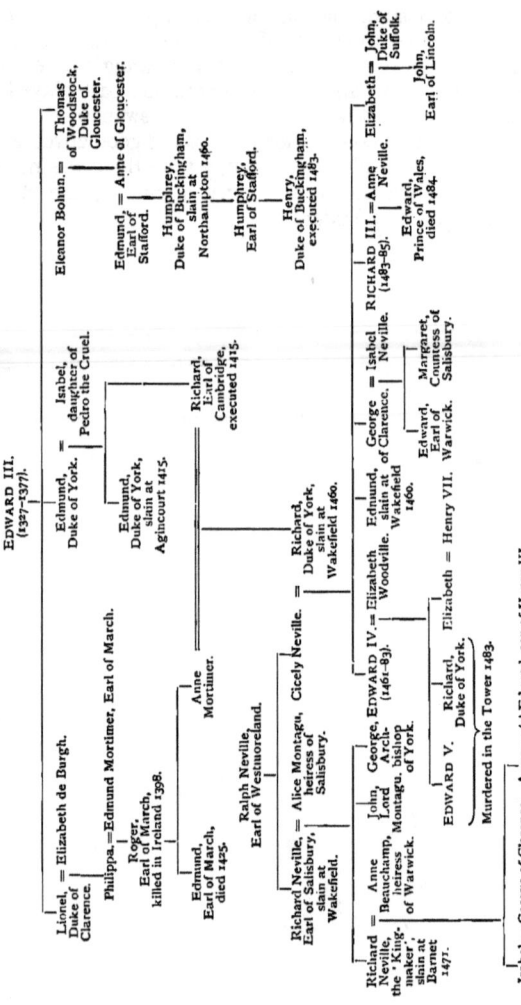

APPENDIX. 161

THE RED ROSE.

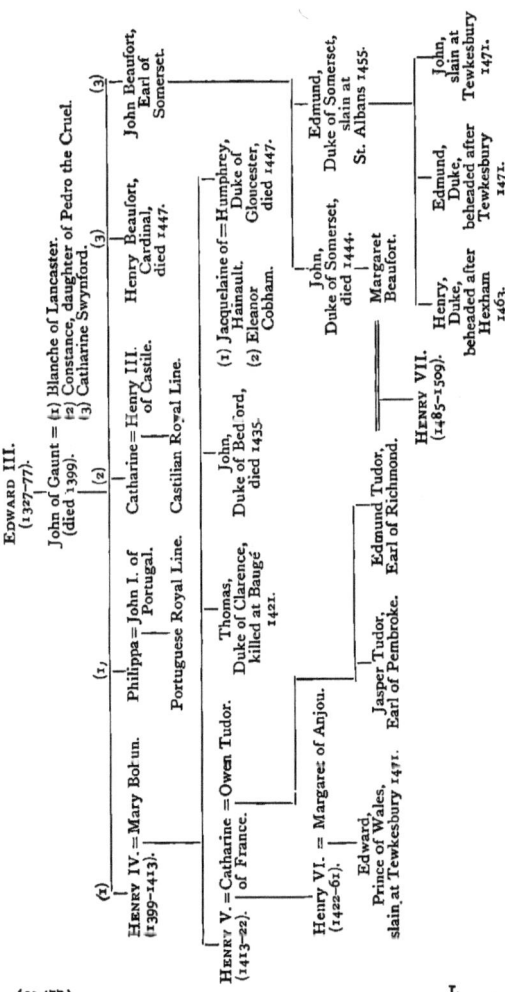

(M 477) L

INDEX.

Agincourt, battle of, 109, 110.
Appellant, the Lords, rising of, 86-88; revenge of Richard II. on, 93, 94.
Aquitaine, duchy of, 52; rule of the Black Prince in, 61, 64; English losses in, 65-69; finally conquered by France, 130.
Armagnac faction in France, 105, 112, 113.
Arras, Congress of, 122.
Artevelde, Jacob van, opposes Louis of Flanders, 23; murdered, 34.
Arundel, Thomas, archbishop, supports Henry IV., 95, 96; persecutes Lollards, 98, 106.
Arundel, Richard, Earl of, a Lord Appellant, 86; impeached and executed, 92.
Auray, battle of, 61.

Ball, John, leads Peasants' Revolt, 81-83.
Balliol, Edward, conquers and loses Scotland, 18-19; at Halidon Hill, 21; struggles of, for Scottish throne, 22, 29, 40; cedes his rights to Edward III., 53.
Barnet, battle of, 146.
Baugé, battle of, 115.
Beaufort, Henry, Cardinal, opposes Gloucester, 117, 123; his death, 125.
Beaufort, Margaret, mother of Henry VII., 147.
Beaufort, *see under* Somerset.
Bedford, John, Duke of, regent of France, 116; his campaigns in France, 117, 118, 121; dies, 122.
Benevolences, raised by Richard II., 93; by Edward IV., 148; by Richard III., 156.
Berwick, taken by Edward III., 20, 22; ceded to England, 53; recovered by James III., 139; taken by Edward IV., 149.
Bible, the, translated by Wycliffe, 90.
Black Death, the, 41, 42; its effects on trade, 43, 59.
Black Prince, the, *see* Edward.

Blois, Charles of, claims duchy of Brittany, 31; slain at Auray, 61.
Blore Heath, battle of, 133.
Bolingbroke, Henry of, *see* Henry IV.
Bordeaux, its loyalty to England, 69, 130; final loss of, 131.
Bosworth Field, battle of, 158.
Bramham Moor, battle of, 103.
Bretigny, peace of, 51-53.
Brittany, war of succession in, 31, 32, 40, 45, 61; expedition of Thomas of Woodstock to, 78.
Bruce, Robert, *see* Robert I.
Buch, Jean de Grailly, Captal de, at Poictiers, 48, 49; defends Aquitaine, 68.
Buckingham, Henry, Duke of, aids Richard III., 151, 153; rebellion and death of, 155.
Burgundy, John the Fearless, Duke of, murders Orleans, 103; allied to England, 104; murdered by the Dauphin, 113.
Burgundy, Philip the Good, Duke of, allied to the English, 114, 116; sells Jeanne d'Arc to the English, 121; abandons the English, 122.
Burgundy, Charles the Rash, Duke of, allied to Edward IV., 141, 145.
Burley, Sir Simon, execution of, 87.

Cade, Jack, his rising, 129.
Cadzand, battle of, 26.
Calais, taken by Edward III., 39, 40.
Cambray, besieged by Edward III., 27.
Cambridge, Richard, Earl of, conspiracy and death of, 108.
Castillon, battle of, 130.
Catherine of France marries Henry V., 114; marries Owen Tudor, 136.
Chandos, Sir John, 56; at Auray, 61; killed in Poitou, 65.
Charles V. of France at Poictiers, 47-49; regent, 50, 51; makes peace of Bretigny, 51; succeeds to throne, 61; renews war with England, 65;

recovers Aquitaine, 65-69; renews war with Richard II., 78.

Charles VI. of France makes peace with Richard II., 88; his madness, 103; makes Henry V. his heir, 114; dies, 116.

Charles VII. of France murders John of Burgundy, 113; proclaimed king, 116; his misfortunes, 117, 118; employs Jeanne d'Arc, 119; crowned at Rheims, 120.

Charles the Bad, king of Navarre, his pedigree, 25; intrigues of, 45, 61, 63.

Charles the Rash, *see* Burgundy.

Church of England, quarrels of, with Papacy, 33; condition of, 74, 75.

Clarence, Lionel, Duke of, 55.

Clarence, Thomas, Duke of, 105; slain at Baugé, 115.

Clarence, George, Duke of, intrigues against Edward IV., 142; exiled, 143; betrays Warwick, 146; put to death, 149.

Clement VI., pope, quarrels with English Church, 33.

Cobham, Eleanor, *see* Gloucester.

Cobham, John Oldcastle, Lord, Lollard chief, 106; executed, 107.

Cocherel, battle of, 61.

Commerce, growth of, under Edward III., 56.

Courtenay, William, bishop of London, his trial of Wycliffe, 76.

Cravant, battle of, 117.

Crecy, battle of, 36-39.

David II., Bruce, king of Scotland, 17; his struggle with Edward Balliol, 19-22; taken prisoner at Neville's Cross, 39; set free, 53.

Derby, Henry (1), earl of, *see* Lancaster.

Derby, Henry (2), earl of, *see* Henry IV.

Disinherited Lords, the, conquer Scotland, 17, 19.

Douglas, Sir James, invades England, 9.

Douglas, Sir Archibald, defeats Edward Balliol, 20; slain at Halidon, 21.

Douglas, Archibald, earl, captured at Homildon Hill, 100; captured at Shrewsbury, 101; slain at Verneuil, 117.

Dupplin Muir, battle of, 18, 19.

Edgecote Field, battle of, 143.

Edward II. deposed, 7; murdered, 10.

Edward III., accession of, 7; his first Scottish war, 10; his marriage, 13; crushes Mortimer, 13; his second Scottish war, 20, 21; his first French war, 23-51; claims French crown, 24; Flemish campaigns of, 27-29; invades Brittany, 32; invades Normandy, 34; victorious at Crecy, 36-39; his naval victories, 28, 44; ravages Scotland, 46; makes peace of Bretigny, 51; his military fame, 56; last years of, 65-67.

Edward IV., victorious at Mortimer's Cross, 137; at Towton, 138; character of, 140; marries Elizabeth Woodville, 141; breaks with Warwick, 142; imprisoned by Warwick, 143; his last struggle with Warwick, 144-146; his French war, 148; executes Clarence, 149; dies, 150.

Edward V., his accession, 150; imprisoned by Richard III., 153; murdered, 154.

Edward the Black Prince, birth of, 13; at Crecy, 36-39; invades Languedoc, 45, 46; victorious at Poictiers, 47-49; marries Joanna of Kent, 54; his Spanish war, 62-64; his troubles in Aquitaine, 64-66; illness of, 66; death of, 72.

Edward, son of Henry VI., born, 131; marries Anne Neville, 144; slain at Tewkesbury, 147.

Edward, son of Richard III.; dies, 156.

Elizabeth Woodville, queen of Edward IV., 141; oppressed by Richard III., 150, 152, 153.

Espagnols sur Mer battle, 44.

Flanders, English trade with, 23, 56; campaigns of Edward III. in, 27, 29.

Formigny, battle of, 125.

France, *see under* names of kings.

Glendower, Owen, his rebellion, 99, 101, 104.

Gloucester, Thomas, Duke of, his expedition to Brittany, 78; intrigues, 84; heads the Lords Appellant, 86, 87; makes truce with France, 88; arrested and slain by Richard II., 92, 93.

Gloucester, Eleanor, Duchess of, 118; condemned for sorcery, 123.

Gloucester, Humphrey, Duke of, Lord Protector, 116; marries Jacquelaine of Holland, 117; abandons her, 118; opposes peace with France, 123; his death, 125.

Gloucester, Richard, Duke of, *see* Richard III.

Guesclin, Bertrand du, aids Henry of Castile, 62; Constable of France, 68.

Halidon Hill, battle of, 21.

Harfleur taken by Henry V., 108.

INDEX.

Hastings, William, Lord, slain by Richard III., 152.
Hawkwood, Sir John, mercenary chief, 56.
Hedgeley Moor, battle of, 139.
Henry IV. (Earl of Derby, Duke of Lancaster), a Lord Appellant, 86; exiled, 94; deposes Richard II., 95, 96; rebellions against, 97, 98, 100, 103; dealings of, with Parliament, 97, 102; latter years of, 104, 105.
Henry V., youth of, 104; his character, 105, 106; persecutes Lollards, 106; invades France, 108; victorious at Agincourt,110; conquers Normandy, 112; made regent of France, 114; dies, 115.
Henry VI., birth and accession of, 115, 116; his character,123; marries Margaret of Anjou, 124; his first madness, 131; captured at St. Albans, 132; takes arms against York, 133; captured at Northampton, 135; again freed, 137; later misfortunes of, 139, 140; restored by Warwick, 145; murdered, 147.
Henry VII., parentage of, 136; conspires against Richard III., 155; victorious at Bosworth, 157, 158.
Henry, King of Castile, his war with Pedro the Cruel, 62-64; his fleet sent against the English, 67.
Heretico Comburendo, Statute *De*, 98.
Herrings, battle of the, 118.
Hexham, battle of, 139.
Homildon Hill, battle of, 100.
Huntingdon, John Holland, Earl of, 85; executed by Henry IV., 98.

Ireland, state of, in fourteenth century, 91; Richard II. in, 94, 95; Richard, Duke of York, in, 127, 134.
Isabella, queen of Edward II., deposes him, 7, 8; her rule, 8; imprisoned by her son, 14.

Jacquelaine of Holland, her misfortunes, 117, 118.
Jacquerie, the, 50.
James I. of Scotland, taken prisoner, 103; set at liberty, 117.
Jeanne, Duchess of Brittany, defends Hennebont, 32.
Jeanne d'Arc, her mission, 119; relieves Orleans, 120; captured and burnt, 121.
Joanna of Kent, marries the Black Prince, 54, 55.
John, King of Bohemia, slain at Crecy, 39.
John, King of France, his campaign in Aquitaine, 34; accession of, 44; defeated at Poictiers, 47-49; makes treaty of Bretigny, 53; dies in England, 61.
John of Gaunt, Duke of Lancaster, *see* Lancaster.
John V., Duke of Brittany, allied to England, 68; makes peace with France, 78.

Kent, Edmund, Earl of, executed, 12.
Kent, Thomas Holland (1), Earl of, 85.
Kent, Thomas Holland (2), Earl of, slain at Cirencester, 98.
Knolles, Sir Robert, invades Picardy, 67.

Labourers, statute of, 43.
Lancaster, Henry I., Earl of, opposes Mortimer, 12.
Lancaster, Henry II., Earl of, wins battle of Cadzand, 26; wins battle of Auberoche, 34; victories of, in Aquitaine, 40.
Lancaster, Blanche of Lancaster, 55.
Lancaster, John of Gaunt, Duke of, campaigns of, in France, 46, 47; marries Blanche of Lancaster, 55; conducts French war, 66, 67, 68; marries Constance of Castile, 67; his rule in England, 70, 71; protects Wycliffe, 76; claims throne of Castile, 85; dies, 94.
La Rochelle, battle of, 67, 68.
Latimer, William Lord, impeached, 71, 72.
Limoges, captured by Black Prince, 66.
Lollards, spread of their doctrines, 90; persecuted by Henry IV., 98, 99; rise against Henry V., 106.
Lose-Coat Field, battle of, 143.
Louis XI. of France, aids the Lancastrians, 139, 144; bribes Edward IV., 148.
Louis, Count of Flanders, adheres to Philip VI., 22, 23; slain at Crecy, 38.
Louis the Bavarian, Emperor, allied with Edward III., 23, 26.
Ludford, rout of, 134.
Lyons, Richard, impeachment of, 71, 72

Manny, Sir Walter, general of Edward III., 32, 56.
Mar, Donald, Earl of, slain at Dupplin, 19.
March, Edmund (1), Earl of, opposes John of Gaunt, 73.
March, Roger, Earl of, recognized as heir-apparent, 89; lord-deputy of Ireland, 91; slain in battle, 94.
March, Edmund (2), Earl of, heir of Richard II., 97, 106, 108; dies, 122.
Mare, Peter de la, speaker of the House

of Commons, 71; imprisoned by John of Gaunt, 73; released, 77.
Margaret of Anjou, queen of Henry VI., 124; leads Lancastrian faction, 125, 128, 131, 134; her victories at Wakefield and St. Albans, 136, 137; flies to Scotland, 139; allied with Warwick, 144; imprisoned by Edward IV., 147; released, 148.
Meaux taken by Henry V., 115.
Moleyns, Bishop, murder of, 128.
Montague, John Neville, Lord, his victories, 140; betrays Edward IV., 144; slain at Barnet, 146.
Montfort, John (1) of, claims duchy of Brittany, 31; imprisoned, 32.
Montfort, John (2) of, *see under* John.
Mowbray, Thomas (1), *see* Norfolk, Duke of.
Mowbray, Thomas (2), Earl Marshal, rebellion of, 101, 102.
Murray, Randolph, Earl of, invades England, 9.

Navarette, battle of, 63.
Neville, importance of the house of, 27; *see also under* Westmoreland, Warwick, Montague, Salisbury.
Neville, George, archbishop and chancellor, 140, 142.
Neville, Anne, marries Edward, Prince of Wales, 144; marries Richard III., 147; dies, 157.
Neville, Isabel, marries George of Clarence, 142; her death, 148.
Neville's Cross, battle of, 40.
Norfolk, Thomas Plantagenet, Earl of, opposes Mortimer, 12.
Norfolk, Thomas Mowbray, Duke of, a Lord Appellant, 86; favoured by Richard II., 92; exiled, 94.
Norfolk, John Mowbray, Duke of, a partisan of York, 127; present at Towton, 138.
Norfolk, John Howard, Duke of, aids Richard III., 153; slain at Bosworth, 158.
Normandy invaded by Edward III., 34; conquered by Henry V., 112; reconquered by France, 125.
Northampton, battle of, 135.
Northampton, treaty of ("the Shameful Peace"), 11.
Northumberland, Henry Percy (1), Earl of, captures Richard II., 95; rebels against Henry IV., 100; second rebellion of, 102; slain, 103.

Northumberland, Henry Percy (2), Earl of, slain at Towton, 138.

Orleans, siege of, 118; relieved by Jeanne d'Arc, 120.
Oxford, John de Vere, Earl of, present at Crecy, 37; at Poictiers, 48.
Oxford, Robert de Vere, Earl of, minister of Richard II., 85; defeated at Radcot Bridge, 86.

Papacy, Edward III.'s quarrel with, 33, 60; corruption of, 74, 90; attacked by Wycliffe, 75; dealings of Emperor Sigismund with, 112.
Paris, surrenders to Henry V., 114; recovered by the French, 122.
Parliament, deposes Edward II., 7; overawed by Mortimer, 11; quarrels of, with Edward III., 30, 31, 70, 71, 73; dealings of Richard II. with, 87, 93; dealings of Henry IV. with, 97, 102; dealings of Edward IV. with, 148; of Richard III. with, 156.
Parliament, the Good, 71.
Parliament, the Merciless, 87.
Patay, battle of, 120.
Peasants' Revolt, the, 79-83.
Pedro, King of Castile, aided by the Black Prince, 62; murdered, 64.
Pembroke, John, Earl of, defeated at La Rochelle, 67, 68.
Pembroke, Jasper Tudor, Earl of, Lancastrian leader, 136, 157.
Percy, Henry (Hotspur), rebels against Henry IV., 100, 101.
Perrers, Alice, impeached, 71; her influence, 73, 77.
Philip VI., King of France, 17; aids David Bruce, 22; his war with England, 25-44; defeated at Crecy, 36; dies, 44.
Philippa of Hainault, queen of Edward III., 13, 40, 71.
Picquigny, treaty of, 148.
Poictiers, battle of, 47-49.
Pole, Michael, William, John de la, *see* Suffolk.
Poll-tax, the, 78, 79.
Portsmouth, sacked by the French, 27.
Praemunire, statute of, 60.
Provisors, statute of, 33.

Radcot Bridge, fight of, 86.
Richard II., accession of, 77; pacifies Peasants' Revolt, 82; oppressed by Lords Appellant, 84-87; his personal rule, 88; vengeance on his enemies, 92-94; his despotic rule, 93; visits Ireland, 91, 94; deposed, 95; murdered, 98.
Richard III. marries Anne Neville,

INDEX. 167

147; his Scottish campaign, 149; his character, 151; murders Hastings, 152; seizes the crown, 153; murders his nephews, 154; his reign, 155-157; slain at Bosworth, 158.

Rivers, Richard, Lord, favoured by Edward IV., 41; beheaded by rebels, 143.

Rivers, Anthony, Lord, imprisoned by Richard III., 151; beheaded, 154.

Robert I., Bruce, king of Scotland, makes treaty of Northampton, 11; dies, 17.

Robin of Redesdale, revolt of, 142, 143.

Roche-Darien, battle of, 40.

Roses, Wars of the, their causes, 126-129; their outbreak, 132; their history, 132-146.

Rouen taken by Henry V., 113.

Salisbury, William Montacute (1), Earl of, friend of Edward III., 13.

Salisbury, William Montacute (2), Earl of, present at Poictiers, 48.

Salisbury, John Montacute, Earl of, a Lollard, 90; supports Richard II., 95; slain at Cirencester, 98.

Salisbury, Thomas Montacute, Earl of, killed at siege of Orleans, 118.

Salisbury, Richard Neville, Earl of, partisan of York, 127; victorious at Blore Heath, 133; escapes to France, 134; slain at Wakefield, 136.

Sawtree, William, martyr, 99.

Schism, the Great, 90; end of, 112.

Scotland, first war of Edward III. with, 9, 10; Edward Balliol in, 17, 19; second war of Edward III. with, 20-22, 39-40; peace with, 53; dealings of Henry IV. with, 103; aids Margaret of Anjou, 139; war of Edward IV. with, 149.

Scrope, William, *see* Wiltshire, Earl of.

Scrope, Richard, archbishop, rebellion and death of, 101, 102.

Scrope, Henry, Lord, conspires against Henry V., 108.

Shrewsbury, battle of, 101.

Shrewsbury, John Talbot, Earl of, his campaigns in France, 120, 121; slain at Castillon, 130.

Sigismund, emperor, his dealings with Henry V., 112.

Sluys, battle of, 28, 29.

Somerset, Edmund Beaufort, Duke of, his campaign in France, 123; misgovernment of, 130; slain at St. Albans, 132.

Somerset, Henry Beaufort, Duke of, Lancastrian leader, 136; executed after Hexham, 139.

Southampton, sacked by the French, 27.

St. Albans, first battle of, 132; second battle of, 137.

St. Cloud, battle of, 134.

St. Leger, Thomas, executed by Richard III., 154, 155.

Stanley, Thomas, Lord, imprisoned by Richard III., 152; betrays him at Bosworth, 158.

Staple, the, company of, 58; statute of the, 45.

Stapleton, Bishop, murdered, 7.

Statutes of Provisors, 33; of Labourers; 43; of the Staple, 45; of Treasons, 45, of *Praemunire*, 60; of Kilkenny, 91; *De Heretico Comburendo*, 98.

Stratford, Archbishop, his quarrel with Edward III., 30.

Sudbury, Archbishop Simon, proposes poll-tax, 78; murdered by rioters, 82.

Suffolk, Michael (1) de la Pole, Earl of, minister of Richard II., 85; impeached and exiled, 86.

Suffolk, Michael (2) de la Pole, Earl of, slain at Agincourt, 110, 111.

Suffolk, William de la Pole, Duke of, minister of Henry VI., 124; exiled and murdered, 128.

Tewkesbury, battle of, 146.

Tournai, besieged by Edward III., 29.

Tours, Truce of, 123, 124.

Towton, battle of, 138.

Treasons, statute of, 45.

Troyes, treaty of, 114.

Tyler, Wat, rebellion of, 79-83.

Verneuil, battle of, 117.

Wakefield, battle of, 136.

Walworth, William, mayor, slays Wat Tyler, 83.

Warwick, Thomas Beauchamp, Earl of, a Lord Appellant, 86; imprisoned, 92.

Warwick, Richard Neville, Earl of, "the King-maker", 127; his exploits at St. Albans, 132; invades England, 134; victorious at Northampton, 135; defeated at St. Albans, 137; victorious at Towton, 138; his northern campaigns, 139; disgraced by Edward IV., 142; stirs up rebellion, 142, 143; exiled, 144; joins the Lancastrians, 144, 145; killed at Barnet, 146.

Westmoreland, Ralph Neville, Earl of, opposes the Percies, 100; captures Scrope, 101.

"White Company", the, 56.
Wiltshire, William Scrope, Earl of, minister of Richard II., 93; executed, 95.
Worcester, Thomas Percy, Earl of, rebellion of, 100, 101.
Wycliffe, John, his teaching, 75; tried by Bishop Courtenay, 76; spread of his doctrines, 90; *see* Lollards.
Wykeham, William of, chancellor of Edward III., 70; his struggle with John of Gaunt, 73, 77; restored to chancellorship, 89.
Wyther, Sir Thomas, murders Lord Holland, 16.

York, Edward (1), Duke of, regent for Richard II., 95.
York, Edward (2), Duke of, slain at Agincourt, 111.
York, Richard (1), Duke of, his French campaigns, 102, 103; leads the opposition, 125, 128, 129; Protector, 132; expelled from England, 134; returns victorious, 135; slain at Wakefield, 136.
York, Richard (2), Duke of, imprisoned, 153; murdered, 154.

Zouche, William de la, besieges Caerphilly, 16.

www.ingramcontent.com/pod-product-compliance
Lightning Source LLC
Chambersburg PA
CBHW070153100426
42743CB00013B/2895